Continued Miracles
Inspiring Testimonies of God at Work in the Lives of Everyday People
Second Edition

by
Debra L. Stout

Continued Miracles
Second Edition

Without journaling

Copyright 2019 by Debra L. Stout
All Rights Reserved

Unless otherwise noted, Scripture quotations are from *The Holy Bible*, New King James Version.
Copyright © 1979, 1980, 1982 by Thomas Nelson, Inc. Used by permission. All rights reserved.

Scripture quotations marked NIV are from *The Holy Bible*, New International Version.
© 1973, 1978, 1984 by International Bible Society.
Used by permission of Zondervan Bible Publishers.

Italicized words in Scripture quotes are the emphasis of the author.

Cover design by Mr. Francis A. Lamoste

While each testimonial in this book is true, a few names and minor details in these first-person accounts have been changed for the sake of anonymity. Some accounts have been edited for the sake of clarity.

Published by Debra L. Stout

ISBN: 9780986174612

Acknowledgments

First and foremost, I would like to thank the Father, Son, and Holy Ghost for an opportunity to serve him. This book is a miracle.

I would like to thank the wonderful folks in Continued Miracles who stepped out of their comfort zone and shared their personal miracle stories with you. They didn't have to. They give honor to God for their miracles. Hopefully you will glean some insight that may change your life positively.

Thanks to all the folks I have met along the way that are too numerous to count who greatly inspired me, and gave insight. This includes but is not limited to: GPCWC Marlene Bagnull, instructors, and Hope Editors' team, official and non-official editors, Dr. Reesa Woolf, and hand chosen reviewers.

A special thanks goes out to the staff at the Cherry Hill Public Library who adopted me as part of the library "family", gave me expert advice, patience, and saw me through to the end.

You know who you are who sent up the prayers. Thanks a million.

Thanks to all the many people who contributed stories and miracle quotes that did not make the final version. Your heartfelt efforts and help are greatly appreciated, have blessed me, and are with me in spirit.

Thank God for you, our readers, who have given the Lord this opportunity to provide you with a fresh ray of hope. My God bless you with a miracle!

Table of Contents

Acknowledgements

Chapter 1: What Is a Miracle?   1

Chapter 2: God's Test of Faith   5

Chapter 3: Dodging Death   19
    Brought Back from the Dead • It Isn't Over 'Til It's Over • Making a Fresh Start • Martin's Grove • Rescued from Drugs • My Delivery Angel • Protected by His Wings • Safe at Home • Simply Amazing

Chapter 4: No Thanks, Addiction   49
    God Gave Me a Second Chance • Free Indeed • God is Waiting for You • Waiting for Daddy • God's Power Demonstrated • My Greatest Miracle from God • Try Not to Die

Chapter 5: God's Favor with Finances   89
    Faith in Action • Eat from the Good of the Land • Forever Grateful • Miracle on Spring Hollow Drive • My God Is Bigger Than My Circumstances • Never Give Up • Supernatural Blessings • Truly a Miracle

Chapter 6: Forgiveness is the Way   115
    Safe in God's Dwelling • Forgiveness

Chapter 7: Divinely Healed for a Purpose   125
    Answered Prayer • An Unexpected Recovery • Cloud Burst • Epileptic Healing • God's Will • I'm Not Ready • Love Conquers All • Loving the Lord Through it All • Radical Faith • Waiting Patiently

Chapter 8: God Works through Animals   155
    Bailey the Yorkie • Bella • Schatzi • The Easter Miracle

Chapter 9: The Miracle of Salvation   167
    Detoured • Breakthrough on Broad Street • God Behind the Scenes • From Prison to Praise • Weigh no More

Chapter 10: Miscellaneous   191
    Holy Trinity House of Prayer • Seeing is Believing

Chapter 11: Write Your Own Miracle Story   195

Chapter 12: Seven Catalysts to Your Miracle   197

Conclusion   199

Endnotes   203

About the Author   205

1
What Is a Miracle?

Anyone who doesn't believe in miracles is not a realist.
— David Ben-Gurion

Do you feel like God has forgotten you? Are you ready to give up? Do you need a miracle?

Don't lose heart—God has been blessing people around the world with miracles, every minute of every day for thousands of years. He continues performing miracles to this day. That's why this book was written—to help you believe God for your miracle.

God wants more for you, however, than simply receiving a miracle. God wants you to seek Him and know Him. He wants to send you blessings. *Continued Miracles* was written to give you a ray of hope and to draw your soul into God's Kingdom. Will you believe, humble yourself, and receive?

Continued Miracles: Inspiring Testimonials

The inspiring miracle stories on the following pages will help you to discover how God severs struggles, breaks strongholds, and destroys destructive paths, leading us to experience His glory. You *can* be set free.

"What about a miracle in *my* life?" you may wonder. We will focus on your miracle stories, too, and explain how to implement seven keys to obtaining your miracle and witnessing God's impact in your life.

What Is a Miracle?

Miracles are special interventions by God on behalf of His people. These supernatural interventions in the ordinary course of nature are a temporary suspension of the accustomed order or an interruption of the system of nature as it is controlled by the force of the Spirit.[1]

Through my research I discovered that miracle stories people share with others represent the tip of the iceberg. Many miracles remain below the radar. Some people keep their miracles private. As I have surveyed people about miracles, I sometimes get the response, "Oh yes, I've had several miracles," yet the person has never shared his story, perhaps wanting to avoid the stigma attached to the miraculous. Could it be that fear keeps people from revealing their miracles?

Jesus continues performing miracles every day. He wants you to be blessed and to bless others by sharing your story. Divulging the drama and details of a miracle story takes a strong and unselfish person. The more your miracle story is shared, the more your transparency will set you free, and the more others will be inspired.

Many of the people in this book who received a miracle have shared their stories openly for the first time, and they have given God the glory. Others tell their stories often wherever and whenever they can. They all have a common goal: to inspire, give hope, honor God, and bring people to a close relationship with God. At the end of this book exercises will help you to record your own miracle.

This edition removes journaling.

Continued Miracles: Inspiring Testimonials

2

God's Test of Faith

We're made for miracles.

— Pastor Ray Barnard

Ken's Story

During my down time, shortly after midnight, I heard in my spirit, "Go to the gym and get in better shape and return to church, for you will serve the Lord."

Alone, I questioned, "Why is going back to the gym so important? It's been ten or more years since I've been to the gym, and I am in pretty good shape. And why go back to church now? I haven't been there for twenty-five years or so, and I think I lead a pretty good Christian life."

I am a New Jersey police officer with a wife and two step-children. I attended church in my early youth with my mother, an example of a faithful Christian. I believed in God and Jesus as the Son of God and my Savior, and I prayed most nights. My mother planted the seed of my faith at an early age.

In my twenties I worked out at the gym as often as five or six times a week, and I lifted significantly more weight than the other men at the gym. At my peak I could bench press 275 pounds in one set of six reps (short for repetitions, single cycles of lifting and lowering weights). But now, in my thirties, I expected to be weaker.

Within a week of my epiphany in the summer of 2009 at the age of thirty-six, I returned to the gym, and in only a few months I reached my former physical prime, bench pressing six reps of 275 pounds in one set. I increased in strength every time I worked out at the gym, eventually reaching heights of strength and endurance I never dreamed possible. My strength amazed people. My wife didn't think it made sense to have increased my strength in such a short time at my age, and my doctor agreed that it was unusual to be nearing my forties and yet be significantly stronger than in my twenties.

Meanwhile, I returned to church and felt at home even after the absence of twenty-five years. The Lord was letting me know I was on the right path. At home I created a small altar for worship. I was on fire for the Lord. Prompted by the Holy Spirit, I started reading the Bible from cover to cover without skipping a word.

I found meaning and significance in little things. Life made more sense as I trusted God. I prayed before going to the gym and tuned in to gospel music and Gregorian chants for my workouts. I knelt to pray after every exercise, thanking the Lord and giving Him the praise and glory. I prayed often at home and in church.

Two summers later I could have passed for an NFL offensive tackle. I bench pressed six reps of 430 pounds in one set, up from 275 pounds two years earlier. I wasn't hitting my plateau, so I kept going and began to reach heights of strength and endurance that seemed impossible. The Lord gave me this physical strength. I believed He had plans for me.

Eventually, I encountered two male angels who stood on either side of me at the gym and seemed to be in charge of my strength training. These "heavenly personal trainers" meant business, so I became laser-focused and serious, too. One night I sensed the angels telling me to go to the gym after working a 7 p.m. to 7 a.m. shift. I told my wife jokingly, "I guess they don't want me to sleep." To my surprise the angels said to me, "This is not a joke." I sensed these angels often, sometimes just before a workout while mentally preparing and frequently during a workout.

One summer evening right before bed, I knelt at the altar in my house praying. Suddenly I heard, "Humble me so I may understand, teach me that I may learn, and lead me so I may follow." All alone I felt perplexed, I had never read those words in the Bible, and no one had ever said this to me, but I believed it was the Lord speaking, preparing me for something.

In July, 2011, I caught a sinus infection that wouldn't go away. It came with headaches and wheezing when I breathed, but the worst symptom was a persistent cough. At times I coughed up to 150 times a day. My family doctor diagnosed it as sinusitis and prescribed antibiotics which I took for a week with no improvement. He referred me to an ears, nose, and throat specialist, who agreed with the sinusitis diagnosis and prescribed more antibiotics, but the cough persisted, and I felt worse. My doctor sent me for a chest X-ray and blood work, and diagnosed me with pneumonia of the right lung. I continued the antibiotics without relief.

In August, 2011, I was examined by a pulmonary specialist who didn't think the X-ray indicated pneumonia. The specialist put me on an anti-inflammatory, performed a CT scan of my chest and later a bronchoscopy (a scope of the lung). When the doctor called on my cell phone interrupting a relaxing chat with my wife with the bronchoscope results, I answered calmly and confidently. I expected him to say everything would be fine since I had never smoked.

"Ken, I wish I could tell you something different," the doctor said, "but your blockage is a cancerous tumor." I silently mouthed this to my wife. Overwhelmed, she ran inside and cried. This upset me. I couldn't move, and stood there alone, shocked, scared, and nervous but not angry at God. I thought, "If I get really ill or die, who will take care of my wife?" I wanted to be the one to care for her, so I focused on what had to be done next to fight this diagnosis. I realized God had prepared me over the past two years for this: stage-four lung cancer. The tumor measured five centimeters in size, and the cancer had spread from my chest to my spine—a shocking diagnosis for a non-smoker.

My mother, a woman of faith, prayed, asking the Lord to heal me. She also asked the Lord to heal her back as a sign of my healing. (Her condition, spinal stenosis, was inoperable, and she suffered every day.) My mother reasoned that if the Lord healed her, He would heal me. Once cured she could help me through my own healing process. Within two days my mother was elated she felt fine.

Continued Miracles: Inspiring Testimonials

As I prayed, the Holy Spirit said, "My son, you will suffer awhile, but you will be healed." I said, "Thank you, Lord," and I felt a sense of peace.

Then, I recalled a conversation with a nurse at the hospital just before my bronchoscopy. I asked her why she wore a blue wristband. She replied, "I am an ovarian cancer survivor. If your scan comes back positive, I suggest you go to the same facility I went to in Philadelphia—the renowned Fox Chase Cancer Center. I knew that was where I should go, so I had the doctors send my data there. I prepared for war against cancer with the help of my doctors and the Lord.

Fox Chase did an MRI of my brain and tested samples of my bronchoscopy as a team of specialists explored genetic testing as a possible source of new medications on the market. The MRI showed three tumors on my brain, and my doctor wanted to start treatments immediately. Devastated to learn that the cancer had spread from my chest to my brain and spine, I still believed that I could be miraculously healed, and I would have the strength to go through the treatments. Surprisingly, I didn't suffer any symptoms from the additional tumors. God blessed me.

I underwent CyberKnife® (a system which delivers high-intensity radiation in a small beam with extreme accuracy) for the tumors in the brain and spine, followed by three weeks of a more standard type of radiation for the tumor in my chest. Once a week during those three weeks, I received low-dose chemotherapy. In October I started full doses of chemotherapy every three weeks.

The five-hour treatments of transfusion chemotherapy left me feeling ill and drained most of the time. The treatments humbled me. I felt afraid of what to expect next.

And yet, I saw a wonderful side of humanity. Family, friends, and even strangers offered me help. I realized that this was one of the lessons I needed to learn, be willing to receive help. As a police officer, I started to lose faith in humanity—and not just at work. It seemed I only noticed the negative things in people.

After my third chemotherapy treatment the tumor in my chest began to shrink slightly. The doctors announced good news: surprisingly and against all odds, testing had revealed that my cancer had a specific signature, an extremely rare characteristic in my type of tumor. This meant I was eligible to take an oral medicine which attacks only cancer cells. Called targeted therapy, this treatment is more effective and has fewer side effects than chemotherapy.

However, the doctor shared some bad news: they discovered more tumor cells on my brain and spine. I wondered, "Were those tumor cells present before, and the doctors missed them, or were they new?" My faith wavered. I knelt down and prayed, "Lord, I know we're not supposed to ask for a sign, but I'm fearful, thick-headed, and stubborn. If it is Your will, and I'm supposed to be healed, please give me a sign I can't dismiss."

A short time later I strolled through the kitchen when all the pots, pans, and canned goods in the cabinets shook. This lasted only a few seconds and turned out to be an unusual earthquake in New Jersey. Was this the sign I had asked for?

The CyberKnife® was used again to treat the newly discovered cancer cells with satisfactory results. The next scan of the chest tumor showed shrinking of the tumor. Treatments progressed without a problem and appeared effective. The doctors allowed me to return to the gym more regularly, and I regained strength. I had never really stopped my workouts during all the treatments, but I finally felt well enough to test my strength again.

The treatment program's success surprised my

mother and the doctors, but my faith suffered. I started feeling depressed, and wondered how and when it all would end. Would I be healed temporarily and die of the disease at a later time? I called my mother, sharing my anxiety, and asked her to pray. Fifteen minutes later, she called back and said, "The Lord led me to a Scripture. Let me read it to you." I couldn't believe what she read from 1 Peter 5:6-11. It matched the words I had originally heard in my spirit. I realized I was being humbled by the Lord and reassured that everything would be alright.

In January, 2012, another set of follow-up scans tested the effectiveness of the new treatments, and the tumor in my chest shrunk to half of its previous size or 2.5 cm. No other tumors remained. In March another scan showed that the tumor had shrunk to 1.5 cm and might possibly be just scar tissue. Two months later, my doctor announced that no active cancer existed in my body. I am one hundred percent symptom-free. Thank God!

I returned to my full-time job as a police officer, able to fulfill all the duties required by the police force. I obtained a medical clearance to run, wrestle, and fight without limitations. Although a specific workout wasn't required, I wanted to be on an equal footing with my fellow officers; I needed to prove I was completely unhindered by the illness. Consequently, I am now stronger than before my diagnosis. I am able to bench press 465 pounds in a set of five reps, by

God's grace, with 500 pounds a real possibility. Caring for my body is vital. After all, I know what it's like to almost lose my life.

Undoubtedly, God healed me for a reason. My perspective at work changed. Although my job as a police officer is to enforce the law, I also realize that God puts people in my path to witness to and help. I want to spend the rest of my days serving the Lord in any way I can, wherever he leads me. I want to go into full-time ministry when I retire.

Reflecting on This Miracle

> *Therefore, humble yourselves under the mighty hand of God, that He may exalt you in due time, casting all your care upon him, for He cares for you. Be sober, be vigilant; because your adversary the devil walks about like a roaring lion, seeking whom he may devour. Resist him, steadfast in the faith, knowing that the same sufferings are experienced by your brotherhood in the world. But may the God of all grace, who called us to his eternal glory by Christ Jesus, after you have suffered awhile, perfect, establish, strengthen, and settle you. To Him be the glory and dominion forever and ever.*
>
> —1 Peter 5:6-11

Continued Miracles: Inspiring Testimonials

Ken's Reflections

Not once during my illness did I say, "Why me?" I thanked God for an opportunity to serve Him in this difficulty. People I don't even know and churches I've never attended put me on their prayer lists. Because I was in great physical condition and had strong faith before my diagnosis, I had the strength to go through the treatments and the faith to believe in a healing miracle. I remember thinking and saying, "I'm a man of faith, my family are people of faith, and I'm going to be fine." I told the doctors, "Do what you need to do. The Lord will lead you. Everything will be fine."

I cast all my cares on God because I knew I couldn't beat cancer on my own. Though wavering at times, I stood in faith, and He blessed me. Our Lord is the healer and only through His grace did I survive.

Yes, I suffered, but today I am able to power lift weights, which is amazing to me. My God-given strength helps me in my job and allows me to protect people on and off duty. I survived a disease that would have killed almost anyone. All of this is possible only because of God's grace.

Even when I had doubts and fears, God reassured me like a loving parent. I know my gifts are from Him, for Him, and through Him, and those gifts have come to me by His will and His will alone. I firmly believe He has much more in store for me. He wants me to demonstrate His love and teachings through my actions. I am a lector at my church, which comprises doing readings from Scripture during the service. I work with the youth group, I am involved in Bible study, and have joined other charity groups. I try to walk as Jesus would in all my actions. Although I can never repay Him for what He has given me, I can do my best to walk worthy of Him. I am nothing special, no better than anyone else, but God gave me a couple of wonderful gifts of miracles, and I will eternally thank Him.

What are you doing when no one is looking? Try to live as free from sin as possible and follow in His ways whether people are watching or not. This is how you will communicate His love and presence. If you get a strong feeling or "voice" prompting you, it may be the Lord. Don't ignore it. The Lord is with you, and He cares. These are the greatest miracles.

Your Response

What would you do if, like Ken, you were diagnosed with stage-four cancer? Would you give up? Would you pray?

Continued Miracles: Inspiring Testimonials

Continued Miracles: Inspiring Testimonials

3
Dodging Death

The Christian religion not only was at first attended with miracles, but even at this day cannot be believed by any reasonable person without one.
— David Hume

Brought Back from the Dead (Evangelist Lorraine)
    I died suddenly in the dining room with 150 people in the next room. While attending a funeral on Ridge Avenue in Philadelphia I collapsed. My pastor and overseer heard the commotion and stopped the service immediately.
They rushed to me and commanded, "Life, come back in her. Life, come back in her." When the ambulance crew arrived, they rolled me out in front of all those people. Everyone was in shock.
    The ambulance rushed me to the emergency room of St. Joseph's Hospital. After I arrived there, an angel of God came to me and declared, "Woman of God, you shall live and not die." Although I lay motionless and couldn't see, I heard those words repeated several times.

Later, I opened my eyes. My thoughts were foggy, and I didn't know where I was or how long I had been unresponsive. I heard Overseer Pratt say, "You are back." He beamed because life had come back into me.

I was admitted to the hospital on December 15, 2010, and amazingly I walked out of the hospital on my own on Christmas Day. My friends and family call me "Mrs. Lazarus." Jesus raised his friend Lazarus from the dead after four days: "Now when He said these things, He cried with a loud voice, 'Lazarus come forth!' And he who had died came out bound hand and foot with grave clothes, and his face was wrapped with a cloth. Jesus said to them, 'Loose him, and let him go.'" (John 11:43–44).

Stepping out in faith for my healing, I have also survived colon cancer for over five years. Surgery was performed, but I declined chemotherapy or radiation.

Reflecting on This Miracle

> But He was wounded for our transgressions, He was bruised for our iniquities; the chastisement for our peace was upon Him, and by His stripes we are healed.
>
> —Isaiah 53:5

Continued Miracles: Inspiring Testimonials

I will bless the Lord at all times; His praise shall continually be in my mouth.

—Psalm 34:1

Evangelist Lorraine's Reflections

When I wrote my name in my Bible in 1997, the words of Isaiah 53:5 were the core of my heart and my beliefs. I still give God the praise for His sacrifices described in those verses. Letting God shine through me is the center of my reason for living. I lost two sisters, three nephews, and four brothers in less than five years. Although I miss them, I know that the only way I can go on is to continue praising God for sending Jesus to die for my sins. One day I will see my family again. In the meantime, I will obey and follow Him. I want Him to know that I love to praise Him.

God saved me for a purpose. Because He wants me to tell others that He sent His Son Jesus, I go into nursing homes and jails throughout the country. It's our duty to tell others of Jesus' saving power no matter what they have done. He can forgive and save them, too. Amen. Be blessed today and always.

Your Response

Evangelist Lorraine expressed gratitude for her miracle by loving others and telling them about Jesus. If you experienced a miracle like Lorraine, in what ways would you express your gratitude to God?

It's Not Over Till It's Over (Jennifer)

I have been described as a vibrant, cheerful woman with a heart for helping people. If you saw me today, you would never guess the ordeal I endured as a teen. Shortly after my eighteenth birthday, a friend and I rode his motorcycle after a picnic in the park on a beautiful spring day in Texas. The picnic, in the park, is the last thing I remember (I learned the details later).

After leaving the park, we passed a mall. A teenage driver, exiting the mall, attempted to cross the busy highway and collided with us. My leg took the brunt of the impact, and the momentum threw me onto the hood of the car and across the median into oncoming traffic. Miraculously, none of the cars hit me as I lay unconscious on the highway, bleeding profusely from a compound fracture in my leg. (My

friend, who was driving the bike, had relatively minor injuries.) A young couple, recent graduates from paramedic school, heard the commotion as they left the mall, and they came running. They assessed the scene, rushed back to the car for supplies, and stabilized me until the ambulance arrived.

Continued Miracles: Inspiring Testimonials

An emergency room doctor phoned my parents in Missouri to tell them what happened. Distraught, they told the doctor the drive would take twelve hours, but they'd get to the hospital as soon as they could. The doctor gently told them not to hurry or drive dangerously because I wasn't expected to survive twelve more hours.

My parents quickly called close family and friends to start a prayer chain. While they drove, the doctors in Texas performed emergency surgery on my leg and started blood transfusions. Alive but comatose, they placed me in a hospital room for continued care.

At one point during the coma, I became aware of a presence in my room, and I opened my eyes. At the foot of the bed, a figure of Jesus stood. He emitted a subtle glow and looked at me with immense love and tenderness. He didn't say anything. I saw this look before from my precious grandmother who helped raise me. I don't know how long He appeared there, but it was profoundly soothing, an experience I can vividly recall even to this day.

Three days later, I came out of my coma. By the end of the second week, I could walk slowly with a walker. I grew homesick, so the doctors allowed me to transfer to a hospital in St. Louis. While the aide pushed my wheelchair to the waiting taxi to go to the airport, I reveled in the beautiful blue sky, the fresh, warm spring breeze on my face, and the singing of the birds. I would never take life for granted again.

My father was a preacher, so God wasn't someone new to me, but it wasn't until the accident that I knew God really existed. Now I have a new awareness of daily blessings. My world transformed from black-and-white to technicolor. I didn't start reading my Bible more, attending church more, or even praying more although I do commune with God now on a much different level. My relationship with God focuses on giving thanks for the many blessings which He already gave me, rather than continually asking for things. I don't feel it is necessary to sit in a pew in order to talk with God—He is everywhere. Knowing that He is protecting me has given me a calm acceptance of life's turbulent times.

Reflecting on This Miracle

> For I know the thoughts that I think toward you, says the Lord, thoughts of peace and not of evil, to give you a future and a hope.
>
> —Jeremiah 29:11

Continued Miracles: Inspiring Testimonials

Jennifer's reflections

Before my accident, I knew *of* the Lord, but I didn't know Him personally. The accident changed my life. Over the years, I have come to understand that if I hadn't had the accident, I would not be the witness I am for Him today.

Your Response

Have you ever had a brush with death? How did it change your outlook on life?

Making a Fresh Start (Mark)

In my thirties I was a musician, living in Stockton, California, with my wife and in-laws. One sunny, summer afternoon, my father-in-law drove about fifty-five miles per hour down the highway in his Mercedes. My wife sat in the front seat near her father, and I sat in the back behind my father-in-law. I doubt that they had any idea what I was about to do next.

For years my wife's family abused me. I couldn't take the suffering anymore, and I decided to end my life right then on that highway. I thrust open the car door and jumped out, hitting the rough pavement at high speed. After rolling for two blocks, I finally came to rest in the median ditch.

Continued Miracles: Inspiring Testimonials

Not only was I suicidal, but now I was all alone. There were no other cars on the road. Even my father-inlaw's car continued down the highway. I slowly climbed out of the ditch and shook myself off, astonished to discover I was unharmed—not a single scratch or broken bone. I knew instantly that God spared my life. Emergency medical personnel who were interviewed later said that jumping out of a moving car at that speed would cause, at the very least, bruises or multiple injuries. Walking away untouched was certainly miraculous.

My father-in-law eventually stopped the car, so I walked along the highway to meet him. Demanding to know why I had done such a crazy thing, he angrily told me to get back in the car. Neither he nor my wife asked if I was injured which further devastated me. I felt like an outsider looking in—all alone with no one to listen. Three years later, my wife and I divorced.

At that point, I made a fresh start. I began to listen more to God's voice than to the voices of other people. This refocusing of my attention gave me inner strength and peace. With God's love I finally came to believe that others cared about me, too. Some years later, I remarried, and we have been married for eleven years.

Continued Miracles: Inspiring Testimonials

I also let God decide the direction for my musical talent. Once I held an impromptu concert in a Sacramento park in order to reach those who wouldn't normally come to church. I shared the story of my brush with death. After the concert, our group reconvened at the church across the street, and many people from the park followed.

At the end of the service, I gave God the glory and asked how many people could identify with my testimony. Then I gave an altar call for those struggling with thoughts of suicide. Twenty-two people indicated they contemplated suicide, and they came forward. Our group prayed and laid hands on them. Several people gave their lives to Christ.

Today, I use my musical talent to glorify God and to be His instrument in changing the lives of others. I never have to go looking for opportunities. God provides them for me.

Reflecting on This Miracle

> If ye then be risen with Christ, seek those things which are above, where Christ sitteth on the right hand of God.
>
> —Colossians 3:1 (KJV)

Continued Miracles: Inspiring Testimonials

Mark's reflections

If you are having similar feelings of suicide, voice those feelings out loud to someone immediately. You need someone to listen to you. Allow that person to come into your world and be your friend. Pray every day. Read the Bible and encouraging devotionals. Spend time with other believers. In time you will gain (or regain) a sense of self-worth.

God has a strategic plan for everyone's life though you may not yet know His plan for yours. Channel your gifting into service for Him, but don't let your gifting, your work, or other people take over your life. Because I trust in God, I have never taken my music out on the road for monetary gain. The Lord gives me the strength to say no to outside opportunities.

Your Response

Have you ever had thoughts of suicide? Have you shared them with others? Based on Mark's experience, how do you think God wants us to respond to suicidal thoughts?

Martin's Grove (Tom)

Martin's Grove and swimming pool are nestled among the trees in a clearing just off Malone's Farm Road.

Continued Miracles: Inspiring Testimonials

Families picnicked, swam, and took in the fresh air of the countryside at the grove. During its heyday, Martin's Grove was not as popular for swimming as Beury's Grove or Reichwein's Paradise Park, but the water was clearer at

Martin's than the muddy lake at Beury's.

One summer day my family enjoyed a picnic at the grove. My mother sat on a bench under a tree. John, my baby brother who had been born a little over a month earlier, lay in his blue baby carriage, covered with white netting to keep flies and other critters away. Pop stood nearby smoking a cigarette. Jane, my six-year-old cousin, was sitting with my mother and helping with the baby.

An eager eight-year-old, I stood by the pool with my five-year-old brother, Bobby. We were wondering what to do since we weren't going swimming. We were allowed to go near the water as long as we didn't get close enough to fall in. As we walked around the pool, I nudged Bobby toward the edge even though I wasn't sure if he could swim. It suddenly occurred to me that it would be fun to push him in. I wasn't being malicious. I was just fooling around. I took another step and gave Bobby a good shoulder hit. That was all it took for him to fall in the pool.

Continued Miracles: Inspiring Testimonials

I saw Bobby smiling at me from the bottom of the pool. His arms and legs seemed to be moving, but it might have been the moving water. Bobby didn't surface. Not sure if there really was a problem, I didn't yell for help. I thought, "If I don't yell or call attention to it, the problem will go away." I looked over my shoulder. A woman I didn't know leaned over the baby carriage to admire John. She asked my mother, "Is this your only child?" Turning to point to the pool, my mother said, "No, I have two older boys over there." But when she looked in our direction, she only saw me, and in a fraction of a second she pushed me out of the way and screamed, "Save my boy!"

With Pop's help, Mom leaned down, reached in, and pulled Bobby from the water. Thankfully, he was still alive. He wasn't frightened, and he still smiled as Mom hugged him tightly. Not knowing I was at fault, she hugged me also. Instead of punishing me, we were allowed to go in the water with our clothes on since Bobby was already wet. Pop drove home to get us dry clothes.

Months later, my mother realized that she had been visited by an angel at Martin's Grove. The angel appeared in the form of an unknown woman asking a seemingly coincidental question, "Is this your only child?"

Reflecting on This Miracle

> When the child grew older, she took him to Pharaoh's daughter and he became her son. She named him Moses saying, "I drew him from the water."
>
> — Exodus 2:10

Tom's Reflections

God is always watching over us. He knows everything, and He acts according to His will, often based on our needs, trust, and prayer.

Your Response

Have you ever seen a tragedy averted through a seeming coincidence? Tell about it.

Rescued from Drugs (Mr. M)

Sitting in a stairwell that reeked of urine, I felt sick and tired. A life on drugs had left me despondent and certain that I was going to die. Rain fell steadily, and I knew I should get to a shelter, but I didn't want to go. Then, I leaned forward and listened. Within my heart I heard God say, "Get up, walk, and get some help."

Continued Miracles: Inspiring Testimonials

This was a divine appointment. The previous year, I had been "dumpster diving" for food and sleeping on the bitter cold ground just around the corner from my mother's house. I didn't care where I was. Survival meant buying drugs, so I begged and stole.

Once, my mother picked me up, drove me home, and let me take a hot shower. What a relief to my aching body! Later, we went shopping, and my mother bought me sneakers, pants, and a warm coat. It was a short-lived transformation. Soon the sneakers had holes like Swiss cheese, my lavender pants turned black, and my coat was dirty and worn with burn marks from sleeping around hot fire cans.

So I sat in that stairwell, knowing I had a choice to make. I could hustle some money, get high on crack, and follow that up with booze to mellow out. Or I could do what God told me. God woke me up even though I didn't know Him.

Wearily, I left the stairwell and walked in the rain several miles from South Philly to St. Joseph's Hospital at 16th and Girard Avenue. When I entered the hospital, I was told that the facility was too crowded, and the staff couldn't help me. "If you can't help me, I'll die," I said.

Continued Miracles: Inspiring Testimonials

The admissions clerk replied, "There's nothing I can do, but you can go to the hospital at 8th and Girard— Giuffre Medical Center." I couldn't give up now. I walked eight more blocks to Giuffre.

In the busy, noisy waiting room of the Behavorial Access Center, the section of the hospital that dealt with drug detoxification, I repeated my plea to the clerk. "If you can't help me, I'll die." There were no beds available, so the clerk asked me to sit down. I met some new people there in the waiting room along with others I knew from the streets. Before I knew it, three days had gone by.

"When was the last time you used drugs?" a nurse asked me. "Three days ago. I've been sitting here for three days," I snapped. The drugs began wearing off.

The nurse had not drawn my blood to test it, but she told me I didn't have enough drugs in my system to require hospitalization. "Are you kidding?" I replied. "This is my life, and if I leave here, I'll die." I wasn't exaggerating about drugs being my life. I graduated from a user at eleven-years-old to one of the top dealers in the city.

Finally, the nurse relented and said, "You can come in and get a bed and a hot shower now." Refreshed, I returned to the waiting room with a clean robe. Someone gave me a baloney sandwich and apple juice, but I didn't feel like eating because I was detoxing. Later, my face broke out in white bumps, and my two back teeth crumbled as I chewed on a straw.

"What's happening?" I asked the doctor.

He replied, "The drugs are wearing off, and they have to come out of your body in some way."

The first night at the center, I slept well with new medicine and plenty of peanut butter and cereal. I stayed there for seven days and grew strong enough to shower without assistance. Attendance at a Twelve Step meeting was required as part of the program. During the first meeting the trainer looked directly at me and said, "One of y'all is going to make it." Determined to end my distress, I declared, "I'm going to be that person."

Reluctantly, I shared my story with the other nineteen attendees. What a relief to go six days without drugs! I now had a ray of hope. When the seventh day came, I didn't want to leave because I was afraid I'd end up back on the streets. I contacted my mom again, and she invited me to stay with her, but I was concerned about staying in her neighborhood. That neighborhood was the heart of where I did all my "dirt"—my drug dealing. With nowhere else to go and

Continued Miracles: Inspiring Testimonials

worried that I would be tempted to use again, I stayed at her house from Wednesday through Friday.

Friday of that week was the best day of my life. My mother gave me bus money to go to my 9 a.m. appointment at Guiffre Medical Center. I had to walk by my drug dealing friends at the corner to get to the bus stop. As soon as I climbed on the bus, I started to cry. Overwhelmed, I didn't want to get high.

I was glad to be admitted to Guiffre for a twenty eight day program on learning to live drug-free. The hospital helped me to get money and welfare checks which they held for me. After the first week, when no phone calls or visitors were allowed, Keith, a consultant from my Twelve Step meeting, spoke at the program. He made such an impression on me that I said, "I want to be just like him." Keith gave me his phone number and said, "Call me." I really appreciated his support.

Darryl, another counselor, also encouraged me. He said, "If you just keep the faith, you're gonna be okay." I didn't know what he meant. On the last day of the program, I was so fearful that I called Keith, and he and his brother came to get me. They took me to get something to eat and then to a Twelve Step meeting across from the hospital where I first went for help.

Continued Miracles: Inspiring Testimonials

The people at the meeting made me uncomfortable. After so many years of using, the thought of being drug free was foreign and overwhelming. In fact, I thought the meeting was a scam. I didn't trust anyone. I looked around the room and was surprised to see Darryl's familiar face.

He said to me, "I knew you were going to be the one to make it. If you stay here in our Twelve Step program and keep the faith, you'll never get high again."

I realized what he meant, and it was another turning point for me. He was right—I never got high again. I'm still clean today, twenty–one years later.

After being drug-free for seven years, I found a good job as a cook in Philly. I was working and paying child support, but I wasn't making it financially. I needed a second job but couldn't find one.

Then, an energetic culinary student named Ron came to the restaurant where I worked to serve an apprenticeship. My boss asked me to demonstrate to Ron how to properly use a knife, and we became fast friends. After our shift that day, Ron asked if I wanted to take a ride with him. I was taken aback and said, "I don't drink." In my past life "take a ride" meant bar-hopping. He didn't know how to respond to my refusal. Finally, I agreed to go with him.

Continued Miracles: Inspiring Testimonials

Ron came whizzing down the parking garage ramp in a new BMW—not exactly the kind of wheels I would expect a student to be driving—and he pulled up in front of me. After I got in the car, Ron said, "I want to tell you something about myself that you don't know." He told me his last name. I didn't recognize the name; it meant nothing to me.

We crossed the bridge from Philly into New Jersey and drove to Mt. Laurel, stopping in a supermarket parking lot. As we were walking to the entrance, Ron said, "This is a new supermarket my family just opened." It was part of a large, well-recognized grocery chain. No wonder Ron had expected me to recognize his last name!

Ron went up to the desk and asked the manager for a job application. He turned to me and said, "We're going to hire you." My eyes got as big as grapefruits as I thought, "This dude's serious." I wasn't aware that God had placed Ron in my life for a reason. Ron added, "I need you to help me with the deli counter, starting on Monday." He introduced me to his father, the owner, before driving me home to Philly.

I was thrilled to start work on Monday at the supermarket at a higher salary than I expected. This was just what I needed — working at the restaurant in Philly during the day and at the deli in New Jersey at night. I hadn't been this happy in a long time.

One night an attractive woman approached the deli, and I started to flirt with her. She stopped me cold by saying, "I don't go out with non-Christian men."

"But I am a Christian," I lied. "Can I have your phone number?" She handed me her business card over the counter. After she left, I changed my mind about calling her and threw the card in the trash. Another evening, two women came up to the counter. One said to me, "I want you to meet my sister." The sister gave me an angry look and blurted out, "I don't want to meet that jerk. I gave him my card, and he never called me."

After a while, she calmed down, changed her mind, and decided to give me a second chance as well as a ride home to Philly. We became close friends. On Good Friday she told me she was going to church, and she urged me to go with her. During the service, it seemed like the pastor's message was directed to me. That night I gave my life to Christ, and I've been attending church ever since.

My encounter with God in the stairwell was a divine appointment. God placed my future wife in the right place at the right time. With her encouragement I began studying for the ministry and became ordained. Now, I no longer live a selfish life. Whatever I do is for God.

Reflecting on This Miracle

> Trust in the Lord with all your heart, and lean not unto your own understanding; In all thy ways acknowledge Him, and he shall direct thy paths.
>
> —Proverbs 3:5

Mr. M.'s reflections

My goal is to help people who are like I used to be. My desire is to point them in the right direction and aid them in turning their lives around. You have to believe that God can get you out of a bad situation. If you hear a small still voice telling you to get up, listen and obey. It's God.

Your Response

On hearing God's voice, Mr. M. walked several miles in the rain to get help. Have you ever heard God speak to you? Did you do what He asked? Tell about the episode.

My Delivery Angel (Sandy)

I was rolling out pizza dough on a Friday afternoon when my water broke. "Well, cancel the pizza for tonight," I

Continued Miracles: Inspiring Testimonials

thought. My pregnancy had been uneventful, so now that it was time to go to the hospital, I wasn't worried. I was pleased our second son was about to arrive.

Because my husband Harry was at work, and my mother was watching our other son, our next-door neighbor Margie and Harry's cousin drove me to the hospital. I contacted my husband on the way and signed in at the admissions office. Nurses ushered me to the labor room where I was connected to an intravenous drip.

I had a blood condition that required a platelet transfusion during delivery to prevent both my baby and me from bleeding to death. Due to some sort of error, however, I was not given an intravenous with platelets. They wheeled me into the delivery room as my labor pains increased in intensity.

As I was waiting for the delivery team to come in, an angel appeared, dressed in bright white. She faced the IV bag and placed her hands on both sides of it. The entire room had a supernatural white aura. In astonishment I asked the angel, "Are those platelets?" The color of the platelet solution should have been red not yellow. "Sandy, don't worry about anything," the angel replied without turning toward me. "Everything has been taken care of."

Then the angel disappeared and didn't return. I was in awe that God would dispatch an angel for me. When the angel left the room, the delivery team took over. I was relieved to have a normal delivery and a healthy baby boy.

Tears streamed down my face and fell on the pillow when I returned to my room. My gynecologist strolled in and asked me, "Sandy, what did you do?" I looked at him, perplexed, and replied, "What do you mean?" He explained that he had reserved a slab in the morgue for me and my baby son. We weren't expected to survive the delivery because I had never received the platelets. We both could have hemorrhaged to death.

The gynecologist suggested that perhaps we survived because of a required medication I had been taking, but I had a different explanation. As he listened intently, I told him of the unexpected appearance of an angel, appointed to rescue my delivery and bring us out safely. "God spared our lives," I said. "I believe my prayers and those of my mom and grandmother and the love of God brought us through."

Reflecting on This Miracle

Again I say to you that if two of you agree on earth concerning anything they ask, it will be done for them by My Father in heaven. For where two or three are gathered together in My name, I am there in the midst of them

—Matthew:18:19-20

Sandy's Reflections

My mother, grandmother, and I prayed all the time during the pregnancy, and I felt fine. Put your trust and faith in God, and you won't have to worry. He'll handle it. Be sure to give God the glory. Share your story.

Your Response

Though you may not have as dramatic a story as Sandy, have you ever had a significant answer to prayer? As Sandy said, share your story.

Protected by His Wings (John)

The car horn blasted long and loud as I jumped back to save my life. At about 10 a.m., my wife and I were standing on the sidewalk of one of the busiest and most challenging streets in Philadelphia—Roosevelt Boulevard.

Part of the Lincoln Highway, one of the first roads traversing America, "the Boulevard" is an historical landmark—a twelve-mile-long, twelve-lane monster running through North Philadelphia. Motorists travel this

Continued Miracles: Inspiring Testimonials

highway dangerously fast as if it is a freeway, even though many parts of it have intersections and pedestrian traffic like any city street. One hundred thousand buses, cars, and trucks plus pedestrians and bicycles travel this highway daily. Statistics show at least three thousand crashes and more than fifty-five fatalities over the last five years.[2]

My car was in the shop for repairs, so my wife and I needed to navigate across twelve lanes of traffic to get to the public bus on the other side. With little sleep the previous night, I hoped I was up to crossing a highway with such a dangerous reputation.

Mustering my courage, I ventured across the first three lanes, successfully reaching the grass median where I caught my breath. I glanced back to see my wife about twenty feet behind me, apprehensively trying to catch up. I crossed two more lanes without any cars coming, but I was so sleepy I didn't realize I was looking in the wrong direction.

Suddenly, a driver in another lane startled me with a blast on his horn. I realized my mistake and headed back to the median. That driver saved my life—there were six cars in the last lane that I hadn't seen. My wife wasn't even aware of what had happened until the horn sounded.

Continued Miracles: Inspiring Testimonials

Eventually, we made it safely across the twelve lanes and got a seat on the bus. What a relief to sit down! After my car was repaired, I was glad not to have to cross the highway on foot anymore. The experience taught me a lesson: keep alert when I drive, and watch out for pedestrians.

Reflecting on This Miracle

He shall cover you with His feathers, and under His wings you shall take refuge; His truth shall be your shield and buckler.

—Psalm 91:4

John's Reflections

Always pray and maintain a growing relationship with God. I believe God protected us. I didn't pray before crossing the street—I just trusted God to get us to the other side. Nevertheless, I don't recommend trying to cross the Boulevard on foot!

Your Response

That timely blast on the horn might seem to some people as mere coincidence, but John is convinced it was a miraculous sign of God's protection. Think over the past several months or years of your life. Can you tell about any "coincidences" that may really have been from the Lord?

Continued Miracles: Inspiring Testimonials

Safe at Home (Sandra)

I was two hours away from home and headed to a small seashore town. The plan was to stay with someone I thought I could trust. I anticipated the evening with the pleasure of enjoying a good visit with someone I liked. Unfortunately, the evening turned out to be different than I expected. Several things happened to make me feel threatened and fearful of my life. I dashed out of the house. On the way out, I grabbed my bag and my wallet which contained only three dollars.

I ran to the bus stop, but the last bus had already gone. Frantic and alone in the dark, and without a phone in an unfamiliar town, I began to panic. But I had recently become a Christian, and I knew I should pray. "Dear God, please help me. What should I do?"

Gathering my courage, I knocked on the door of a nearby house to ask for help, but the people turned me away because they didn't know me. As I approached another house, a man, just pulling into his driveway, was kind enough to call the police. What a relief! I hoped the officers would help me somehow, but I wasn't prepared for what happened next.

To my amazement, God did something totally unheard of—He sent me a series of private escorts. A state trooper drove me part of the way home. Then I transferred to another state trooper's car, and he drove me a little farther. Finally, a police officer from my town drove me the last leg of the journey to my front door. This was a miracle, and it really boosted my trust and belief in God. With a grateful heart I poured out my thanks to God when I got home.

Reflecting on This Miracle

That you may be sons of your Father in heaven; for he makes his sun rise on the evil and on the good, and sends rain on the just and on the unjust.

—Matthew 5:45

God is our refuge and strength, a very present help in trouble.

—Psalm 46:1

Sandra's Reflections

Just when you think there may not be a way out, God can show up and show off.

Your Response

Continued Miracles: Inspiring Testimonials

Sandra was in a tough situation—it was too far to walk home, and she had no phone, almost no money, and no transportation. What would you have done? Would you trust God to get you home?

Simply Amazing (Dan)

While stationed in Vietnam, I wore a cross I'd fashioned from heavy metal. It was about a half an inch thick. During combat, the chain broke, sending the cross to the ground. I picked it up and put it in my shirt pocket next to my heart. As the battle continued to rage, a bullet hit the cross—dead center over my heart—and knocked me to the ground. My chest felt warmer than usual. A medic saw me go down, rushed over, and checked on me. "You lucked out," he said. "You're gonna be okay." The force of the bullet had bent the cross but left me relatively unharmed. Having the cross in my pocket saved my life.

Reflecting on This Miracle

> But as for you, you meant evil against me; but God meant it for good, in order to bring it about as it is this day, to save many people alive.
> —Genesis 50:20

Dan's Reflections

God's always there when you least expect it.

Continued Miracles: Inspiring Testimonials

Your Response

What would you do if this were you? Would you see God's protective hand?

4
No Thanks, Addiction

Miracles are a retelling in small letters of the very same story which is written across the whole world in letters too large for some of us to see.
— C. S. Lewis

God Gave Me a Second Chance (Reggie G.)

My mother was a strong God-fearing woman who tried hard to instill God's Word in me as a child, but I just couldn't resist fun. A good-looking guy, I got a lot of attention from girls which also made me popular with the guys because I developed a reputation as a Casanova. From early on, I liked being in the spotlight. Studying challenged me because I couldn't resist when friends stopped by my window and called me to have some fun.

As I grew older, my friends started applying themselves to sports, schoolwork, and hobbies, but I sought out things that gave me immediate satisfaction—and long term repercussions. I got involved in drugs, smoking, and drinking even though I considered myself a born-again Christian.

Continued Miracles: Inspiring Testimonials

Mother's Day, 2009, was a turning point for me—and one of the worst days of my life. The bottom fell out. I was laid off from a job where I made good money. Although I qualified for unemployment, that benefit eventually ran out, and I wondered how I would survive. In hindsight I realize that God allowed me to lose that job.

I lived a sinful life for thirty-seven years—drinking, drugs, and women, all of which boosted my ego. Life was a speeding train that was going off track. Eventually, I couldn't weather the storms, and I hit rock bottom. That's when God gave me a second chance after those thirty-seven long years of addiction to cocaine.

Bad circumstances forced me to grow up and evaluate my life. I knew I had to change and move on to a higher level in my relationship with God. He was faithful in His love and care for me. God gave me a game plan and directed me to stay in His lane. As my walk with the Lord became more consistent, I started seeing the light of the glory of life. He enriched my life more and more, and I began to see favor from God. I couldn't disconnect myself from the Lord at this point.

I was fortunate to get into a Christian rehabilitation program in Camden, New Jersey. While in the program I attended different churches in the area with my counselors, but I hadn't found the right one. Something was missing in my life, and I hoped God would put me on a new path.

I began attending a church in Philadelphia where the pastors, who were skilled in the Word of God, practiced what they preached and had a heart for people. Hungry for the Word, I arrived early each week and sat in the front seat with my notebook and pen, eager for the anointing of the pastor. Excited with God's message and the pastor's delivery, I joined the church on the spot. God revealed to me the path He wanted me to take. I took the new members class and didn't miss a single one. They were a priority for me. Upon graduation three months later, I sensed that God was empowering me.

Things began looking up after that. I got a new job on a Monday, and Tuesday I got the title to my car—just in time, too, because the tow truck was coming to haul away the car for expired registration. You should have seen the look on the driver's face when he saw me waving at him, my new tags in hand!

Each time the pastor mentioned a Scripture reference in a sermon or Bible study, I hurried to write it down. When I went home, I looked up the Scripture in my Bible and applied it to my life. I felt good about developing a positive lifestyle.

Continued Miracles: Inspiring Testimonials

The enemy fought me, however, and tried to get me to go back to my old ways. God needed to remove the worldly garbage out of me. Even though I was a Christian and attended church, disobedience dominated several areas of my life. One night I went down to my favorite bar, expecting to party with some people I knew. To my surprise, the Lord spoke to my heart: "Get out of this bar!" My eyes grew wide. God's direct communication with me was startling. Immediately, I motioned to the bartender, paid him, and left.

Although I wanted to be further ahead in developing my new life, I had to learn patience. Change doesn't happen overnight. I stood in line after Bible studies to buy the tapes, so I could listen to them at home in my quiet time. I wanted to replay the messages and remember the Word, not just listen to it. If you play church, you won't reap anything. I wanted to apply what the pastor spoke.

The Holy Spirit gave me a burning desire to learn. I listened to the Word of God on Christian television each week and took notes. I bought Christian books and listened to Christian radio stations. Relentless, I vowed, "Nothing is going to stop me. The devil stole my life for many years. Not anymore." I began to take tithing seriously, making sure I gave ten percent of my money each week to the church.

Continued Miracles: Inspiring Testimonials

The worst is over, and the best is yet to come. God totally delivered me from thirty-seven years of disaster, drug demons, wrong companions, and the stronghold of constant smoking. God put a vision in my heart. As I began trusting Him, His Word started working. I didn't get derailed trying to work out all the details myself.

I have been blessed with an opportunity to serve at a church doing outreach—serving hundreds of hungry people each week—while maintaining my class schedule at church. I stay in God's lane, and He provides for me. Bible classes are a priority for me and not an option. I expect to keep taking classes at church whenever they are offered.

I am new from the inside out. I'm energized, and I'm expecting to be a world changer.

Reflecting on This Miracle

> But without faith it is impossible to please Him, for he who comes to God must believe that He is, and that He is a rewarder of those who diligently seek Him.
>
> —Hebrews 11:6

Continued Miracles: Inspiring Testimonials

For You, O Lord, will bless the righteous; with favor you will surround him as with a shield.

—Psalm 5:12

For the Lord God is a sun and a shield; the Lord will give grace and glory; no good thing will He withhold from those who walk uprightly.

—Psalm 84:11

Reggie's Reflections

God took me the long way, like the Hebrews in the Bible, so I could handle the good things he has given me. My companions have changed—I can't hang with the same people I did before. God brought me new friends and happiness. He is my provider, and since I trust in Him to take care of me and my needs, I'm blessed to be able to tithe twenty percent—double what I am called to give back to God.

The enemy is still my enemy, but I don't agree with him or give him any room to throw anything at me. The clock is ticking, and this is not the time to get lukewarm. Commitment to the Word of God and to a new life is necessary. Read the Bible—it's an everyday thing. You don't have to do it on your own power. The Holy Spirit will help you.

I now have supernatural peace, patience, and self-control, which I could never get on my own. I am so grateful for God's grace. God did not die on the cross in vain.

Your Response

Reggie learned that a new life in Christ meant a clean break from certain people, places and practices. What are you willing to sacrifice to have the life you desire?

Free Indeed (Mr. D)

I was a married man living in the Philadelphia area and working in corporate America. My life appeared to be normal and successful. I went about business as usual every day, but I was living with a secret. I was desperately trying to break free from a lifestyle of cocaine use and homosexual behavior.

In 1985, I decided to get tested for HIV. *Will I get AIDS? Do I already have AIDS?* These questions plagued me. I was devastated when the blood results came back positive. It may sound incredible, but, in spite of all this, I was a believer who knew the Bible and attended church. After getting my diagnosis, I prayed through Psalm 91, a warfare psalm. After saying these verses out loud, I heard the Lord say to me, "You will be all right." Even though I heard this, I felt the need to confide in a Christian friend. My friend did not judge me for what I had done. She showed compassion and love and gave me words of encouragement, as well as Scriptures of comfort. Most of all, she prayed for me.

I also read the book *God's Medicine* by Kenneth W. Hagin. Mr. Hagin wrote about how God healed him of an incurable disease while he was bedridden as a teenager.

The end of the book provides a list of Scriptures on healing. I confessed these Scriptures out loud daily and eventually memorized them. Each time I went to the doctor, I expected the results to be negative, but they were always positive. Thankfully, however, nothing in the results indicated I had full-blown AIDS.

Later, I wrote to a prominent pastor out of state. The pastor prayed and wrote back to me. I was encouraged to get the letter but stunned at his response. He said I was trying to conquer my drug addiction on my own instead of letting Jesus do the work. I thought that if I recited Scripture many times, I would receive the manifestation of a healing. I wanted to do the work, and I wouldn't let the grace of God operate.

Continued Miracles: Inspiring Testimonials

I wanted the issue resolved, so I did not give up. A Christian doctor examined me. He felt that the original test should be repeated along with a more advanced western blot test. The routine blood test results came back positive, but the western blot test came back negative. This only caused me more confusion and anxiety. Each time blood results came back, I snorted cocaine, but the following day, I always confessed Scripture.

Finally, I shared my test results with my pastor, a godly man who sought the Lord in prayer before discussing the subject with me. He confirmed the comments of the previous pastor and added more. He told me to stop looking for the promise in the test results and just take God at His word.

I decided to do the two tests once more. This time both results came back clean, but, instead of rejoicing, I decided I wasn't worthy of these good results because I had not done enough to deserve the clean diagnosis. Feeling low, I snorted cocaine again because it was my coping mechanism. I used cocaine once every three or four months over the last two years of my battle with drugs, despite going to work every day, despite praying and attending church.

I decided to consult a third doctor who performed more tests. Because I didn't like the results he gave me, I returned to the Christian doctor who had conferenced with other experts. They concluded that I had built up antibodies to the HIV virus. I didn't have and would never get AIDS.

My relief and freedom from fear did not change my low self-esteem. At this point, I listened to a Christian teaching tape series entitled "Faith Righteousness." The basic premise of the series was that Jesus did it all on the cross for us, and it was finished. The main Scripture mentioned on the tape was, "There remains therefore a rest for the people of God. For he who has entered His rest has himself ceased from his works as God did from His" (Heb. 4:9–10).

About a year later, I was free from cocaine. I am glad to declare that I haven't touched it for sixteen years. Now, I am free indeed.

Reflecting on This Miracle

> There remains, then, a Sabbath rest for the people of God; for anyone who enters God's rest also rests from his own work, just as God did from his.
> —Hebrews 4:9-10

> For a righteous man may fall seven times, and rise again, but the wicked shall fall by calamity.

Continued Miracles: Inspiring Testimonials

—Proverbs 24:16

Now to him who is able to do exceedingly abundantly above all that we ask or think, according to the power that works in us, to Him be glory in the church by Christ Jesus to all generations, forever and ever. Amen.

—Ephesians 3:20-21

Mr. D's Reflections

Cease from your own work. You can't do this by yourself. Any work you do is an extension of what God told you and the fruit of what you believe. You should not try to perform to make yourself better because God finished the work in Jesus. He did the work for you. Stop trying to do it by yourself.

It has been sixteen years since I was delivered from drugs and homosexual behavior. From time to time, I struggle with homosexual pornography. But I know that through the blood of Jesus God will take the desire away in the same way He delivered me from cigarettes and cocaine. Even though I fall, I still get back up and fight round by round, inning by inning, quarter by quarter.

I never took any HIV drug therapy, and yet I never got AIDS. I am healthy, whole, and secure in the finished work of Jesus Christ. If God can deliver me from my torment, He can do the same for you. If you are still bound, would you like to be set free?

Your Response

Have you ever struggled with an addiction? Did you try to break free in your own strength or by trusting God? Are you still struggling?

God Is Waiting for You (Virginia)

I would have done anything to hear a loving word from my mom as a child. She was a good mother to her seven children, but I didn't think she loved me. Feeling rejected, I looked for love and approval from other people and other things. If I even thought that someone might reject me, I ended the relationship. I began lying and manipulating people.

At age fourteen one of my sisters and I were placed in foster care in Philadelphia. We were abused physically, mentally, and sexually. Eventually, we were taken to another foster home which was just as traumatizing. One day my sister and I bolted down the stairs and out the door of our foster home. We found our way back to our family's home, but I endured more physical and mental abuse there.

Continued Miracles: Inspiring Testimonials

Longing to please my mother in spite of the abuse, I cared for the five children, cooked, and cleaned, and I did it all without being asked. One afternoon when my mother came home, I glanced her way, looking for some appreciation, but she went straight to bed without noticing my efforts. Rejection resurfaced.

At sixteen I became pregnant, and the child's father rejected me. Looking for acceptance, I hung out with other teens, smoked marijuana to fit in, and led a double life, willing to be or do whatever they wanted. My beautiful baby daughter was born, but I didn't know how to give her love or be a mother to her. One day, my mother asked me if I wanted her to watch my nine-month-old daughter for a couple of hours, and I agreed. I didn't return home until my daughter was two-years-old.

I graduated from marijuana to heroin, and soon I became addicted. An attractive teen, I worked at a modeling studio that was a front for prostitution. I felt accepted because my boss lauded me with constant praise and recognition. Eventually, however, the drugs took a toll on me, and I lost my alluring appearance. I no longer looked like the woman who first started at the studio. My boss displaced me, insisting I needed to get a different job. Anger came over me and I felt like a failure. Rejection resurfaced. Without many work skills I turned to the streets for my livelihood, and I was locked up repeatedly for prostitution. Although I wanted to make money to take care of my daughter, I developed an addiction to crack cocaine instead.

During one incarceration my grandmother and mother were contacted, and they drove to see me at the women's prison in Philadelphia. When I informed my mother that I was working as a prostitute, I was totally embarrassed. My grandmother, a God-fearing woman, prophesied over me.

She told me that an evangelist said I was going to bring many souls into the kingdom of God. I looked at my grandmother and replied, "Are you crazy? There is no way I'm going to bring anyone to God." I was headed in another direction, angry at God and myself.

"Did you bring the bail money?" I asked. Instead of responding to my question, my grandmother gave me a list of psalms. Even though I was running from God, I memorized the Scriptures and placed them in my heart. To this day I still remember them.

Prison was a revolving door for me, one that lasted for twenty-five long years. When I was released, I went back to the streets and to rejection, abuse, manipulation, people pleasing, and shame. Once I didn't sleep for three or four days in a row which sent me into seizures, and when I woke up, I didn't know where I was. A stranger told me I didn't belong in that place, and my first response was to ask him where my money and drugs were.

Eventually, I used fifteen bags or more of heroin and cocaine every day. I overdosed nine times and was pronounced dead twice. I hoped the drugs would kill me because I wanted to die. Usually, I woke up with someone reviving me. But God poured out His grace and mercy on me.

One day I was sitting at a crack table, and I felt clearly that it would be my last time using drugs. I knew somehow that God was going to rescue me. You see, every time I had been arrested, I attended church services and learned more of the Word of God. In fact, I ministered the Word of God to two people before they died in a crack house, and when they both accepted Christ, I knew that I had a calling on my life. That day at the crack table, I cried out to the Lord and asked him to take away my addictive lifestyle. I looked to heaven and told God I didn't want to continue this lifestyle, feeling the hurt, pain, shame and guilt. I prayed, "God, give me the life you sent me here to live."

Later, while in prison, one of God's servants ministered to me. I attended the prison's church service, and back in my cell, God spoke to me. This time, with a sincere heart, I asked God to forgive me.

One day a guard announced that a prison ministry was coming to hold a service, and the first fifteen people to sign up could go. I asked for permission too late, so I was number sixteen on the list, but when I pleaded to go to the service, the guard let me attend. The minister gave his testimony which immediately captured my attention. I continued reading my Bible when I returned to my cell.

When the time came for me to be paroled, I asked instead to be transferred to an in-patient rehab program. God opened that door for me, and I completed the program successfully.

I have a heart for helping others overcome the same challenges that I suffered for so many years. Now, I counsel inmates through a church prison ministry as an ordained evangelist. One of my goals is completing my GED degree and encouraging those in prison to do the same.

Reflecting on This Miracle
I can do all things through Christ who strengthens me.

—Philippians 4:13

Your Response

Virginia turned to God for help after years of rebellion, how did He respond? What does that say to you about your situation?

Waiting for Daddy (Debra Ann)

This day was going to be the best—my daddy was coming to pick me up! I was fifteen-years-old, and I hadn't seen my father in years. Although I had a good life at home, I loved and trusted my father and missed him very much. From time to time I asked my mother why she and my daddy didn't stay together, but she wouldn't explain.

I was looking forward to the change of being with my dad because, recently, I had not been happy with my life. While living on military bases around the country with my mother and step-father, I was well-respected as a leader, but once we moved to New Jersey, I struggled to fit in. I couldn't wait until I turned sixteen so I could quit school. I didn't like following rules.

My mother begged me not to go with my father, but I was certain that visiting him was going to be great. I was overjoyed as I ran down the steps, hopped in my father's Eldorado, and took off with him to the motel where he was staying.

Continued Miracles: Inspiring Testimonials

After having fun in the pool, I changed into one of dad's yellow shirts because my clothes were wet, and I hadn't brought a bathing suit. I met dad's business partner and his girlfriend who was not much older than me. They seemed nice.

Later that day, I watched my father pull out a small aluminum packet and lay it on top of the dresser. He opened it, exposing a snow-white powder that he asked me to sniff with a straw. Naive and trusting, I did as I was asked, not at all understanding what would happen next. My father sniffed some of the powder too. My nose stung a little, and I was light-headed as I lay on one of the two double beds and relaxed, watching television.

Then my father closed the curtains which made the motel room quite dark. I didn't understand why he closed them so early. I was shocked with what happened next.

I lay on the bed, devastated, with tears streaming down my face. *Why would my father defile me like this?* The anguish was more than I could bear. I bolted for the bathroom, locked the door, and turned on the shower to drown out the sound of my tears. My father knocked at the door, asking if I was all right. Apparently, he didn't think he had done anything wrong. This was the first day of my descent into hell.

Continued Miracles: Inspiring Testimonials

Day in and day out, my father kept me high and in bed. What should have been the best years of my life would last decades and include drugs, prostitution, pregnancies, robbery, and jail time. My father entered and re-entered my life several times. He seemed to have a spell over me.

Lured by his promises, I joined him on a road trip to Florida. But by the time we reached Richmond, we had run out of money, so my father sent me into a hotel to look for a "customer."

Since it was my first time at solicitation, I didn't know what to do. I just looked around uneasily, my heart racing. I was very uncomfortable when a man approached me, but I had no choice. We needed money for food and gas.

When I returned to the car, my father praised me as I silently handed him the money. I was furious and refused to look at him. *How could he do this to me?* I thought. Disgusted, I dreamed of being back on the military base as a child, eating my mother's cookies.

Tired of living out of the Eldorado in Florida, I was horrified every time he sent me into a hotel to prostitute myself.

By the time I was seventeen, I was still in Florida and homeless more times than I could count. I was the mother of a one-year-old who was in foster care, and I had another child on the way. Although I loved my son, I knew I wasn't able to care for him by myself. I drank, went clubbing, prostituted myself, and stole for survival. During this time, I was far from home, and I felt I was all alone, but my aunt was praying for me. She served as a long distance support team. There were also a few people who helped me along the way.

While selling my body, I never knew where I might be headed next. My father offered a false ray of hope by leading me to believe he wanted to help me and my son. But instead of spending time with both of us, he insisted I leave my baby son with a relative in New Jersey while he and I went out for what he said would be a short while. He had devised a plan to hook me and take me back to Florida.

One warm Florida night I sauntered into a night club. I had decided to run out on my father. I met an older man at the club and went home with him. After living with him for a while, I discovered he had a girlfriend. "Stay away from my man!" she yelled at me as she threatened to kill me. I became instantly homeless.

A few years later I was living with another boyfriend when my father re-entered my life again. Dressed in an old mink coat, he told me he was a millionaire, and he could make my life better if I followed his instructions. (At the time, I had a sewing job, and I was receiving a monthly welfare check.) But once again, my father was able to lure me away—this time with a promise of big money. I took my sons to my sister and followed my father, only to discover that he had developed a plan for us to rob banks using false identifications.

Eventually, I got away from him again. I held various jobs periodically. One particularly good job was at a nursing home with seniors. As a certified nursing assistant in my thirties, I managed to pay my bills and rent. I attended church with my grandmother and diligently read the Bible although I wasn't totally committed to the Lord yet.

Imagine my surprise when my father called me from federal prison. He never told me why he was there. I hadn't heard from him in a few years, and I listened cautiously to him. Before I realized it, he pulled at my heart strings again and smooth-talked me into a get-rich-quick scheme. In my search for a better life and still wanting my father's love, I left my Christian lifestyle and my son and followed my father after his release from prison. I immediately fell back into my old ways—partnering with my father, snorting cocaine, and robbing banks in three different states, hoping I wouldn't get caught. This wasn't what I had in mind when I dreamed of a better life.

Continued Miracles: Inspiring Testimonials

The defining moment for me came after my father severely beat me one day while we were living in Indiana. I was afraid to remain with him but also afraid of what the next phase of my journey would be. Finally, I broke the devil's hold over me. I decided I had had enough abuse and couldn't continue. I severed the relationship with my father for good and headed for New Jersey.

Devastated, homeless, and rejected by my family, I made my way back to New Jersey on a bus. I knew it would take time, and it wouldn't be easy, but I was committed to re-establishing a relationship with my sons and my mother.

I turned myself in to the New Jersey police, thinking that at least in jail I could get a clean, comfortable bed. Little did I realize that there had been a nationwide search for me. I was a fugitive from the law in three states. Devastated when my sentence came down, I was still glad I had broken my bond with my father even though I felt like I was doing time for his crimes. After all, he had planned the bank robberies.

Unlike my fast-paced life on the road, time passed slowly in the New Jersey prison system. After I had been incarcerated for quite a while, I asked about my release date, hopeful that I would be released soon. I was shocked to discover that, without advance notice, I would be transported to two other jails on the East coast to serve terms there as well.

I made a concerted effort to turn my life around while in prison. I focused on following the rules, doing my work, and completing my GED which I was pleased to receive. Since I didn't want to spend one more day than necessary behind bars, I was on good behavior. Once, I picked up some comic books to look at because I love art and cartoons. Another inmate grabbed them back and threatened to break my neck. I was glad that I didn't react and do anything that might jeopardize my release date.

I realized that I needed a way to survive in jail. I specialized in survival on the street for years, but I knew now that I needed supernatural help. God knew I was out of options, and I didn't like to follow rules. Since I couldn't bear losing my freedom, I dropped to my knees on the cold concrete floor and called out to Jesus as my grandmother taught me. I earnestly prayed the sinner's prayer, asking God to forgive me of my sins, and dedicating my life to Him. It was finally time to give up my past, to live drug and alcohol free. God gave me a second chance.

While I was serving my final prison sentence, the Lord answered my prayers and turned my life around. I watched a Christian television station and related to the message presented by one particular pastor. I read the Scriptures and attended Bible studies with the guards who showed me favor, as did some of the other inmates. I truly wanted to live a Christian life as I had done with my grandmother. To relieve my stress in jail, I used my talent as an artist to design and sell custom note cards for others.

God freed me from the bondage which held me captive for so many years, and I overcame my long-term fear of being alone. My buried wounds were so deep only Christ could reach me. I am so glad I accepted Christ. God chose me to fulfill His purpose even in prison.

Once out of prison, I lived with my grandmother who accepted me unconditionally. I have since been reunited with my mother and my sons. Today, as a wife, mother, and grandmother, I reach out to women nationwide, encouraging them to trust God to give them hope, a new mind, and a new heart.

Reflecting on This Miracle

> For the Lord does not see as a man sees; for man looks at the outward appearance, but the Lord looks at the heart.
>
> —1 Samuel 16:7

Continued Miracles: Inspiring Testimonials

Debra Ann's Reflections

The Lord is coming back for a church without a spot, blemish, or wrinkle. If your heart is spotted with hatred, He's not coming back for you. Anything less than forgiveness will kill you. Why let the other person win over you for the rest of your life? I waited for Daddy, my heavenly Father, and I wasn't disappointed because His love never fails.

Once I was at the lowest point in my life and had nowhere else to turn, I had to trust God. Jesus went down to the lowest part of the earth and came up with all power in His hands. There was no question of trusting God. When I put my faith and trust in the Lord and prayed for discernment, He gave me the gift to see whom I could trust where man was concerned. Finally, able to let go and let God, I felt safe and secure in His arms.

How can you trust something you cannot see? My answer is that feelings come from within you. So you must trust in the Lord with all your heart and not lean on your own understanding and feelings. If God can blow breath into dry bones (Ezekiel 37:1), he can certainly mend the brokenhearted and set the captives free. To God be the glory!

Debra Ann's full story can be read in her book: My Daddy, the Devil, and Me

Continued Miracles: Inspiring Testimonials

Your Response

God gave Debra Ann the power to forgive her father, despite his years of abuse. Are you harboring hatred and unforgiveness in your heart right now? Do you need to forgive someone?

God's Power Demonstrated (Mr. R.)

I was exposed to pornography and molested by my uncle at five or six-years-old. At eleven-years-old I was exposed to pornography again by my stepfather. By snooping in drawers or digging through the trash, I found plenty of pornography in magazines. By the age of thirteen, I hung around with older guys and became promiscuous with various girls and guys. My stepfather and I tried to imitate the porno movies we watched. Addiction to pornography became my lifestyle, my way of escaping reality.

Because my mother and stepfather argued constantly, I felt there was very little love in our home. A late-life baby for my mother, I didn't think she wanted me. I felt abandoned and rejected. I never met my real dad who was in the military and moving around the country. I sought love and acceptance in all the wrong places. Alcohol, drugs, and sex met my needs and killed the pain.

Continued Miracles: Inspiring Testimonials

My friends offered me marijuana. "Come on. It won't hurt you," they said. Since I wanted to fit in, I followed their lead and got high. By fourteen I was addicted to cocaine. I went from marijuana to cocaine to crack.

Eventually, I became homeless. To find a place to sleep, I often broke the glass windows of empty hotel rooms, stepping over glass shards as I snuck inside. I slipped out by the crack of dawn. But most nights I slept outside on the dirty, hard ground.

To support my habit, I broke into cars and stole radios, or I robbed from stores or my family. One time I stole my mother's food stamps which really made her angry. Another time, I moved in temporarily with a homosexual man, just for a place to stay. But I hated the trade of sex for safety, and I left after two days.

Finally, I had enough of the daily danger and drama. I dragged myself to the Salvation Army, and they gave me a warm meal. While there, I heard the gospel and received Jesus as my personal Savior. I had been to church before, and I knew how to pray, but I had strayed away from the Lord. Without a mentor whose positive values might move me forward, I refused to accept help and go to church. When I came into the center one day with my knife, I was asked to leave. I went right back on the streets.

Continual death threats from drug dealers kept me watching my back, and within five years I was tired of this life of fear. Complicating my health problems, I broke out in boils all over my body. By this time I also had a child on the way, and I didn't want my child to grow up without a father. God used my baby and the death threats as a way to change my heart. The Lord said, "If you don't surrender, you will die in the streets. Your daughter won't have a father." I got down on my knees and surrendered my life, asking God to take away the drugs and alcohol.

A television commercial prompted me to seek out a nearby rehab facility. I walked to the facility and enrolled in the program. During the rehabilitation I lived with my grandparents. I found my grandmother's Bible and started reading it, and I started praying. My faithfulness in reading the Bible, attending church, and pursuing the rehab program every day shocked the family.

When my beautiful daughter arrived, I lived near her and her mother. My daughter's mother saw the changes I made in my life. We began a new relationship, and eventually we married but it was like traveling down a rocky road. Even though I was now delivered from drugs and alcohol and had more peace of mind, I never resolved my abandonment and rejection issues. Whenever my wife and I had an argument, I sought comfort in pornography because my fantasy world wouldn't reject me.

As God revealed my sick behavioral patterns to me, I felt guilty and ashamed. God showed me why I was doing what I was doing, and I cried out to Him for help. But because of my unresolved issues, the problems with my wife escalated, and eventually we divorced, creating a fresh dose of abandonment and rejection.

Incredibly, God used the divorce to heal me and deliver me from those issues. He never left me nor abandoned me during my difficulties. I was able to break free of pornography because of God's love, and I am now happily married to the woman of my dreams, my Cinderella.

Isn't God amazing? Freedom from the bondage of alcohol, drugs, and homosexuality for several years uplifted me. I don't need to carry a knife for protection. God protects me from my enemies. I enjoy sleeping in a comfortable bed and not on the ground. I continually ask God to give me strength, and I read my Bible regularly. I don't want to affect my teenage daughter or my wife with any sin.

Things are going well now. My family goes to church routinely. I launched my own business, and I look forward to a bright new future with my family. God is restoring my life, making me whole and complete.

Reflecting on This Miracle

Be sober, be vigilant; because your adversary the devil walks about like a roaring lion, seeking whom he may devour.

—1 Peter 5:8

Abstain from every form of evil.

—1 Thessalonians 5:22

Mr. R.'s Reflections

God is the center of my relationships now. If you surrender everything to God, He can take the pain and tragedy away and create something beautiful of your life. You may think God can't forgive you, but He can, and He isn't shocked by your sins. He's waiting for you to surrender.

Choose your friends wisely. Be very careful about the companions with whom you hang out. Don't get started with pornography—or if you're already in it, don't let it have the victory in your life. Turn to God.

Your Response

When we are trapped in a sinful habit, it's often because we are trying to drown out a deep, aching pain that

God wants to heal. Mr. R. was only able to be free of pornography when he surrendered the pain of rejection to the Lord. Do you have a sin in your life that seems to keep hanging onto you? What do you have to surrender to God?

My Greatest Miracle from God (Bob)

A magazine caught my attention over ten years ago and planted a pornography seed in my heart, leading me into a danger zone. My interest grew, and, like many other men, I started viewing pornographic videos of women. Pornographic thoughts became deeply rooted and well developed. When DVDs came out, I was buying them like crazy, maxing out my credit card. Unexpected, unwanted debt became a worry.

As technology progressed, magazines, marketed with pornographic DVDs inside, were readily available on many store shelves, and no longer behind a counter. Initially, the cost for such magazines was twenty to thirty dollars. As supply and demand increased, the price dropped. I purchased three packs of magazines for seven dollars every few weeks.

I had a good time, but I was hooked.

Unfortunately, these DVDs generated a growing desire for more pornography. Pornography became an addiction. It dominated my thought patterns, and I suffered more depression, loneliness, and guilt. I felt trapped like a fly in a spider's web. There appeared to be no way out of my secret.

Before long, my thoughts escalated to a higher level, and I fantasized that I was the man in the movies. This continued day after day for years.

Eventually, I realized that I needed to find a way out of my addiction because I became disgusted with myself and guilt-ridden. Supposed to be a born-again Christian, worldly ways dominated my life. I became what the Bible calls "backslidden," which means to relapse into bad habits or bad behavior. I decided that this was not the lifestyle for me anymore.

One day I took a major step and surrendered to God. He answered and took me gradually through a process to remove my sinful desires for pornography. First, I confessed my sin to God. I decided to take the next step allowing the Lord to change my sinful thought patterns.

Years before, a Christian television program made an impact on me, and I wondered if it was still being broadcast. One day, as I was flipping channels, I discovered a religious television channel with many good programs. One show in particular appealed to me because it addressed the need to change our thought patterns. God sat me in front of the television at the right time. At the end of the show, I ordered the home study package, including a variety of books.

As I took the initiative to complete each day's assignment, I started seeing progress. Many Scriptures were referenced during the program, and I faithfully searched my Bible for them. My desire for pornography steadily decreased although it was not totally gone. What really made the difference and led to total deliverance was reading my Bible I purchased daily even if for a short period of time and putting what I read into my heart. I read Christian books as a steady diet. I attended an informal Bible study each week with a couple of friends and brought along a notebook to take notes. I mustered the courage to share my secret and was given several Scriptures on temptation. I looked them up and quoted them out loud to myself. I got stronger every day.

Reflecting on This Miracle

> If My people who are called by My name will humble themselves, and pray and seek My face, and turn from their wicked ways, then I will hear from Heaven, and will forgive their sin and heal their land.
>
> —2 Chronicles 7:14

Continued Miracles: Inspiring Testimonials

Bob's Reflections

Today I am free from this sin that had me bound for years. Finally, I found the peace of mind for which I hoped. I successfully emerged from this spider web with God's help.

Be careful of anything out of the ordinary on your emails, especially if it mentions a woman's name. One day my sister got an email while researching Arabian horses on the internet. She got a reply email on Arabian horses, but instead of getting details about the horses, the email was a pornographic site. Emails may look innocent, but they can still lead to pornography.

This was my introduction to pornography. Just like any credit card purchase, you don't see the consequences until later. With pornography or any sin, there is a saying that holds true: pay now or pay later.

You have to take the first step. Put your trust in God and His words in the Bible. His Word really is a two-edged sword. I use the Amplified Bible which is easier for me to read. If you don't have a Bible, get one and read it. If you have a Bible, pray that the Lord will give you wisdom, knowledge, and understanding of the Scriptures. Read and reread passages on temptation. Find a church that you feel comfortable attending. If I conquered this sin, considering how long I had the temptation, anyone can—with God's help.

Your Response

How do you handle temptation and sinful behavior?

Is your method anything like Bob's?

Try Not to Die (Scott)

I grew up attending church every week until I was about seven-years-old. My grandmother had a heavy influence on my early walk with God, but by the time I was thirteen, I became a problem child, getting into trouble continually. I dyed my hair blue, wore facial piercings, and always acted tough. My temper was short and volatile. I listened to Marilyn Manson albums, read books on witchcraft, and even prayed to the devil. In retrospect, I am sure I invited demons into my heart.

Arrested by fifteen, I served my first state sentence of six to eighteen months at Renaissance House in Newark, New Jersey. It was scary walking up to the door of that place for the first time, not knowing what to expect, but that fear wasn't as bad as what I went through later. I hated getting on my hands and knees to scrub the floor with a toothbrush or facing the wall for hours until they told me I could move. But Renaissance House did provide me with treatment for addiction and counseling on how to realign my life.

Only a year after my time at Renaissance House, I spent nine months in an extensive rehabilitation program, and an interruption occurred when a friend and I ran away to Brooklyn. Because I violated that program, the authorities drove me to the Jamesburg, New Jersey, Training School, a medium-security facility for juveniles where I would spend another year. The kids called it "Gladiator school" because there were brutal fights every day. If you didn't fight, you were labeled a weakling, and the other inmates tortured you from then on. I sharpened my survival skills at Jamesburg.

I was housed in one large room with about fifty other guys. Quarters were tight, so I slept with one eye open, and my radar always on. Nevertheless, I got into a couple of fights. Once, the other guys stomped on me and smashed my head into the toilet, knocking me unconscious. Blood splattered everywhere, and I had to get stitches. I hated being there.

When I was released, I hit the ground running. I had the time of my life—living fast, partying, and doing drugs with my friends. While incarcerated, I met some new people who always talked about shooting cocaine. They gave it rave reviews. Back on the streets again, I asked a friend to take me to Camden, New Jersey, to get some cocaine so that I could see what it would do for me. But after I arrived in Camden, I wasn't sure I wanted to go through with my plan. Did I really want to put a sharp needle in my arm? At the place where we picked up the drugs, I saw a sniper on the roof, guarding his territory—in broad daylight, in the middle of the day. *Do I really want to be here?* I asked myself again.

I followed my friend who got the stuff, and we walked behind a smelly, disgusting dumpster so we could shoot up. I watched him take off his belt and wrap it around his arm. He told me to do the same. I couldn't do it. Here I was in the heart of the ghetto behind a dumpster. I didn't have the stomach to take my belt off and wrap it around my arm. We left and headed to a better spot on the railroad tracks where I eventually got my courage and shot up.

Years later, with a full-fledged addiction I was sent to jail several times. My addiction to cocaine and heroin worsened, costing me more money and more anxiety. I suffered the despair and uncertainty of homelessness, and I found myself in crack houses with scary people. Suicidal, I missed my family and friends.

Throughout my problems and difficulties, God was calling me. Countless times He tried to get my attention, and eventually I couldn't ignore Him. Finally, He allowed me to be locked up in a jail where I met a man named Paul who became my friend and workout partner. We discovered that we had similar experiences with God trying to get our attention. We started going to Bible studies when the announcement was made over the loudspeaker.

A cool guy named Dan ran the Bible studies. A wise man, Dan helped us grow in faith, answered our questions, and broke difficult Scriptures down so we could understand them. Paul and I underlined and discussed Bible passages frequently.

In jail I finally gave up and came to Christ. The Holy Spirit changed my way of thinking and opened my eyes to my really sinful nature. Convicted even about small things, I began to recognize the evil in my life and the evil done by the human race. I started praying every night.

After my release I kept in contact with Paul and attended more Bible studies with Dan. In prison I realized Jesus had a purpose for my life. Everybody I talked to about God told me I should share God with others because I have a good way with people.

One summer morning around 4 a.m., I started pacing back and forth for two hours outside of my home because I had a backache. I didn't know that someone saw me. A well dressed lady approached, handed me a small Bible tract, and left. She sensed I had a spiritual need.

After I read the tract, I tried to locate the lady. When I found her, I introduced myself. She seemed surprised to see me again. I told her I had read the tract, and she smiled. We spoke briefly, and I gave her a quick overview of my story. Then I asked her, "Can we do a Bible study tomorrow?" She and her friends agreed to help me.

The next week I went to Bible study with them. God's Word was exactly what I needed to hear. Eventually, I even went to church with them. During the sermon, the pastor looked right at me and described my situation. I was amazed. At the end of the service when he asked if anyone wanted to be saved, I raised my hand. God was speaking to me, right on time.

Reflecting on This Miracle

Thus says the Lord to you: for the battle is not yours, but God's.

—2 Chronicles 20:15

And now abide faith, hope, love. These three, but the greatest of these is love.

—1 Corinthians 13:13

Continued Miracles: Inspiring Testimonials

> Trust in the Lord with all your heart. And lean not on your own understanding; In all your ways acknowledge Him, and He shall direct your paths.
>
> —Proverbs 3:5-6

Scott's Reflections

Recognize any signs that you are being sucked into an addictive lifestyle, and recognize God's call when He wants to bring you home. Jesus came to heal the sick, and He can heal you too. Without Jesus there is only emptiness and death. Many of my friends died in their addictions. Pain is the only thing that can be found at the end of the syringe. Don't live your life hooked on a poison. The only way to joy and happiness is to be sober and to live for Jesus Christ.

Your Response

Why do you think Scott wandered away from God when he was younger? Do you know anyone who is wandering like Scott? What could you say to someone like him?

5

God's Favor with Finances

Expectancy is the atmosphere for miracles.
— Edwin Louis Cole

Faith in Action (Dolores)

For two years my daughter Courtney and I shared one car, but life was getting complicated. We desperately needed a miracle for another car. My sister was my backup driver whenever Courtney needed our car for her job, but now August was approaching, and my sister would be starting back to college. I would no longer have a way home from work. Because of some poor financial decisions in the past, my credit was bad, and I doubted I could get a car loan.

Our pastor preached a series on "Outrageous Faith" with an emphasis on Hebrews chapter eleven. "Now faith is the substance of things hoped for, the evidence of things not seen" (Hebrews 11:1). The pastor stressed that we should do our part and give God something. So I stepped out in faith to seek a car for Courtney but to no avail. My faith wasn't where I knew it needed to be. I felt like a failure.

Throughout the series the pastor impressed on us that any person could believe when circumstances were going well in his or her life. But when times are hard, it's difficult to believe. Having faith is more than just believing. Faith is evidenced more clearly when it is put into action rather than when it is just spoken. Each week the focus for the service was about having faith, and I was strengthened after hearing the Word. Each week of the series a different member of the church shared how God had worked on his or her behalf. Each person had stepped out in faith, and blessing had followed . . . a new car, a new job, a raise, or a promotion.

When one of our church members purchased a new car, God directed me to ask for the name and phone number of the salesman. I put my faith into action by making the call, but doubt made me fearful. Still, I followed the instructions of the salesman to get approval over the phone for a car. Surprisingly, I later received a call from a different salesman in the dealership, a believer. God wanted him to work with me. The miracle had been set in motion.

Five days later Courtney and I drove to the dealership, intending to purchase a car for Courtney, but God had a different plan. The salesman asked me if I was looking for a car as well to which I replied, "Yes, I'm open." We filled out the paperwork and patiently waited for God's miracle to materialize. Fear tried to come over me again, but I began reciting silently to myself, "For God hath not given us a spirit of fear; but of power, and of love, and of a sound mind" (2 Tim. 1:7).

I texted my pastor and asked her to pray for all to go well. She texted back and told me to start worshipping God. Silently, I told God I loved Him, and I thanked Him in advance for what He was doing. I quoted more Scripture: "If you ask anything in My name, I will do it" (John 14:14). "For the Lord God is a sun and shield; the Lord will give grace and glory; no good thing will he withhold from those who walk uprightly" (Psalm 84:11).

After I started worshipping God, the salesman came back and informed us, "We're finishing up the paperwork on your car," and he handed the keys to me. Twenty minutes later he returned again, looked at me, and said, "We're detailing a second car."

Amazed, I blurted out, "Are you serious?" "Yes," he replied, smiling.

"This is a miracle!"

Our salesman replied, "The finance manager just

said the same thing: 'It's going to take a miracle to get two cars.'"

God performed a miracle right before our eyes. Not only was my car approved by the bank, but two additional banks approved a loan for each car.

A second part of the miracle happened a week later when I received letters from several other banks. Each letter stated my credit score which increased on each letter I received. God was improving my credit right before my eyes.

Before my miracle I felt like I didn't deserve a second chance because of my previous financial mistakes. But God knew our need, and He provided the cars when we needed them the most.

Reflecting on This Miracle

> Now faith is the substance of things hoped for, the evidence of things not seen.
>
> Hebrews 11:11

Dolores' Reflections

This miracle increased my faith so much. I realize that serving God is not about the materialistic things we have or desire, but God can use any situation to increase our trust and belief in Him. Through His miracles, I have had an opportunity to share a testimony of victory with others.

God is able to do anything we ask, but we must ask in faith. We have to do our part and not sit and wait for God to do it all. We have to give Him something to work with, meaning we have to do the leg work and position ourselves in a posture of expectancy. We cannot doubt. It is so important we know God's Word, for in times when doubt and fear try to make us waver, we can believe in God's Word and His promises that He will never leave us or forsake us.

I shared my miracle story with my immediate family, my church family, my co-workers, and now with you. I thanked God before and after the miracle, and I still do every day as I get in my car and see my daughter get into hers. I get emotional because I know it was only by God's grace that I had another chance at re-establishing my credit. This has also been a great opportunity for Courtney to start establishing credit.

Now my daughter and I are able to drive to church, bless others by bringing them to church with us, and get to other places during the week. We feel safer because we are driving cars which are in good condition. We are now able to improve our credit which will open other doors of opportunity for us.

Your Response

What do you think of Dolores' story? Would you have made the same decisions if you were in her situation?

Eat from the Good of the Land (Sharese)

The Lord launched me out into the deep by having me leave my job and go into full-time ministry for the first time. I knew He had a plan for me. Still, I had a home and a mortgage to pay and repairs on the house became necessary. What was I going to do? I relied on my faith and trusted God fully to raise support for my ministry and for basic needs.

One evening I was in the bedroom when I sensed a presence near the doorway. Stunned, I discerned that this was not an evil spirit. I asked God, "Lord, who is this presence?" I saw an angel in a white robe with a gold sash, possibly male, who had a book in his hand. He flipped the pages which were all blank.

Curious, I asked the angel, "What's in the book?"

He replied, "God's re-writing your story." He now had my full attention because I was leaving everything familiar and starting out new in full-time ministry. Then the angel disappeared. I was relieved and blessed. The Lord had honored me with this appearance of one of his ministering angels. I went to bed with the knowledge that God was looking out for my best interests.

My concerns about repair costs on the house continued though. One problem was the attic fan which wouldn't work. Some donations had been given, but they were short of the total time required for this repair.

Usually, I listed the donations with the required information and forwarded the donation list on to our organization. But something was not correct in my tally. There seemed to be additional money. Had I forgotten to count some of the donations? I was compelled to look under the bed to recheck the donation money, and to my surprise, a sum of money appeared which I hadn't placed there. Was I going crazy? Where did this money come from?

I asked the Lord, "Lord, please reveal to me who sent this money." God replied that He had sent the money to me as a gift. Amazed and encouraged, now I could have the ceiling fan repaired. Praise God! He delivered . . . just in time.

Elated, I called my pastors and shared my story with them. A year later I'm now in full time cross-cultural ministry and discipleship, and I am totally reliant on the Lord as my Provider for all my needs.

Reflecting on This Miracle

> And the Lord shall supply all your need according to His riches and glory by Christ Jesus.
>
> —Philippians 4:19

Sharese's Reflections

Many times we rely on our own initiative to raise the support we need. God knows what we need before we do. Have strong faith. Pray to God, cast your cares on Him, and rely on Him to provide your needs. He doesn't always provide the way you want Him to or in your timing, but start trusting in the Lord with all your heart. Don't concern yourself with the past. If I can rely on the Lord to provide for my needs, you can too.

Your Response

The appearance of money is indeed a miraculous and unusual answer to prayer. Why do you think God chose to answer Sharese's prayer this way?

Continued Miracles: Inspiring Testimonials

Forever Grateful (Alisha)

One fall day, I ran out of food and money to feed my young children, even though I was on welfare. I didn't know how I was going to feed them. Then I remembered Psalm 37:25 which says, "I have been young, and now am old; Yet I have not seen the righteous forsaken, nor his descendants begging bread."

Before the end of the day, someone from my church blessed me with food and money. I shouted for joy and gave thanks to God for keeping His promise to me.

On another day I was sitting on a bench watching a woman hand out tracts. We had never met, but I had seen her before on a few occasions. This particular day the Holy Spirit directed me to sit next to her. She asked me, "Do you believe in miracles?" I replied, "Yes, I experienced one," and I proceeded to tell her my story, giving honor to God for His continuing support.

Reflecting on This Miracle

> I have been young, and now am old; Yet I have not seen the righteous forsaken, Nor his descendants begging bread.
>
> —Psalm 37:25

The Lord is my shepherd; I shall not want.

Continued Miracles: Inspiring Testimonials

—Psalm 23:1

Alisha's Reflections

Believe and trust God. My family and I offer a prayer of grace before we eat our meals, And every night before my children go to bed, we pray - Psalm 23.

Your Response

Alisha trusted God to be Jehovah-Jireh, her provider, and He wasn't late. Would you be able to trust God in a situation like this even up to the last minute?

Miracle on Spring Hollow Drive (Dan)

My family of seven had outgrown our three bedroom home in Delaware. The home we desired was a new-construction of 10,000 square–feet with six bedrooms. However, my wife and I faced several obstacles if we were to own a new home.

The real-estate dealer told us we would need $35,000 to hold the lot, but my wife and I were going through bankruptcy and didn't have the resources. We asked if the real estate dealer could hold the lot for us until the end of the month. We were prepared to pay $5,000 down and the balance upon the sale of our old home. God showed us favor. The real-estate dealer said she would write up a contract, and my wife and I wouldn't have to pay anything until we sold our home. The Lord spoke to our hearts and told us to "sow" $5,000 (in other words, give it away to certain people whom God would reveal to us). I believe God gave us this test to see if we would trust Him to obtain the home for us. We sowed the $5,000 in March, and the journey began.

The new home should have been ready the previous December, but it was now March. After the sale of our old home and the clearing of the bankruptcy, my wife and I pulled our credit report. We wanted to see where we were for the approval process. Our credit score was 450—not good. However, due to the conditions in the industry and permits required, there was a delay in the approval process.

Two months before in January, I had been working for a Fortune 10 mortgage company that closed when it went under investigation. I lost my job. I was paid my last year's salary average for the next six months. The Lord asked me where I placed my trust—in the wages from my old job or in Him.

"In You, Lord," I replied. He also asked if anything was too hard for the Lord. "No," I said.

I signed the mortgage contract and stepped out on faith. Unfortunately, I became fearful, and I wavered. I decided that I didn't want the house. I wanted my money back. The next day the builder asked me for a mortgage contingency. The contingency stated that if I was not approved for the home then I would forfeit the $35,000. The pressure was on.

That same day my wife took the kids to a baby shower, and I had the day to myself to think and pray about the situation. God directed me to Hebrews 10:38, "But my righteous one will live by faith. And if he shrinks back, I will not be pleased with him." This changed my mind.

Shortly thereafter, my wife and I joined a new church. The pastor was preaching on faith. His messages helped to boost my trust in God.

God used another event in my life at this time. I was in a barber shop when God put it in my heart to give the barber $500. I gave the money out of obedience to God. I learned later that the man's car had been repossessed.

Within two weeks God again put it in my heart to ask the builder to pay for my closing costs because of my lack of income. The real-estate dealer said the builder would not pay all the costs, but he would pay $12,500. I gave away that $500 to the barber, and God showed me favor.

Everyone in the family was excited. We took pictures and walked on the property, praying, and believing that this

Continued Miracles: Inspiring Testimonials

housing opportunity would work in our favor. Our credit score went from 450 to 670, a much healthier score, in seven months. We applied for the mortgage and received approval. Everything seemed to be going smoothly.

One week before the house settlement, the mortgage company changed the rules and required us to put an additional $70,000 down. Fear overcame me again. Our family had immovable faith. We had to come up with $70,000 or go to another mortgage company. We chose to use another mortgage company, but since the offices were closed for the Thanksgiving holiday, we had to wait for an answer on Black Friday.

I cried out to the Lord. God told me that when I moved into our new home, I should remember that we did not get the house like everyone else by relying on salaries to pay the costs. On Monday my wife and I were approved for the mortgage. We went to settlement the next Tuesday. The builder honored his word and gave us $12,500 toward our closing costs. The Lord instructed us to sow (give) $5,000 as a thank offering to the church. Thanks to the Lord, our family moved into our new six-bedroom dream home on Spring Hollow Drive. We never let the obstacles stop us.

Reflecting on This Miracle

> Is anything too hard for the Lord? At the appointed time I will return to you, according to the time of life, and Sarah shall have a son.
>
> —Genesis 18:14

Dan's Reflections

Nothing is too hard for the Lord. All things are possible to him who believes. Obedience is required. Nothing is impossible with God.

Your Response

Have you ever been impressed by God to give away a significant amount of money—an amount it seemed you could not afford? What did you do?

My God Is Bigger than My Circumstances (Sharon)

With the confidence that God had a purpose and plan for our children, my husband and I prepared Myles, our middle son, for college. We invested in summer classes to give him a taste of the subject area that had always been of interest to him—the world of robotics and engineering.

During his junior year in a New Jersey high school, we moved in with extended family to help them avoid foreclosure on their home. The plan was to sell our home and purchase our relative's home, but things didn't work out as expected. Although my husband and I had the right intentions, our house didn't sell, so we ended up pouring out every asset we had to maintain two mortgages and double utilities. We came to a breaking point, and a decision had to be made immediately. We returned to our own home, in debt and uncertain of our future.

To compound matters, my husband was laid off after twenty-six years of service, and we eventually filed for bankruptcy. With our oldest son in his last year of college, we struggled to pay his tuition and keep our house.

Myles was about to graduate from high school, and he hoped to attend Drexel University's school of engineering in Philadelphia. As all parents do, we hoped for scholarships. Myles was accepted by all three colleges to which he applied, but he was adamant about attending Drexel. He was invited to attend an informational day at the university, and we accepted, but when we received the financial aid package, we were disappointed to find it only covered ten percent of the entire tuition.

Based on our circumstances, there was no way we could afford the tuition, but we accepted the initial offer. As orientation day approached, I wanted to share with my son that we couldn't afford a college with tuition of $52,000 a year. But when I looked at the excitement in Myles' eyes, I couldn't bring myself to break the bad news.

As we traveled to the college, I felt guilty. I was going there under false pretenses. While strolling around the campus, Myles held his head high, never doubting for a minute that he might not be attending the school. He had faith that God was working behind the scenes on his behalf.

The first speaker at the orientation, the director of financial aid, welcomed everyone. I remembered her saying that if anyone had questions to feel free to speak with her. But I was hesitant to approach her.

Myles remained confident, assuring me that this was where he belonged. I talked with God silently, asking Him why I had brought my son here and set his hopes high just to shatter his dream. I walked over to the financial aid office to see if there was anything else that could be done. Their response was not promising.

As we descended the stairs from the financial aid office, I saw the look of disappointment on Myles' face. Our past financial mistakes were going to prevent us from giving our son what he wanted and had prepared for. "NJIT (New Jersey Institute of Technology, his second choice and a less expensive school), here I come," Myles mused. He was really discouraged, but he didn't want me to feel badly.

Continued Miracles: Inspiring Testimonials

Angry, I believed the situation was beyond hopeless. When we got to the bottom of the stairs, I saw the woman who opened the orientation having a conversation with someone. Myles and I reluctantly headed out the door. As we started to walk outside, the Holy Spirit directed, "Turn around and go speak to her."

We continued walking and I questioned, "Lord, what am I supposed to say to her? I'm not going to tell her my business." But the Holy Spirit spoke to me again and insisted. I shared this with Myles. "Mom, if the Holy Spirit said this to you," he replied, "then let's go back in."

We went back in the building, and the director was available. Relieved, I approached her and introduced Myles. I told the director that this school had always been on the top of our list, but the financial aid offered was not nearly enough for him to attend. She asked why, and I realized this was my opportunity to share our situation.

The director said she would keep Myles' name on her desk, and she advised us to send an appeal letter to request additional funding for Myles' tuition. After fifteen minutes, we said our good-byes. We submitted the appeal letter, and two weeks later we received a letter from Drexel. The university offered to pay ninety percent of the tuition through grants and available funds. Myles could pursue his dream at the college of his choice.

My family and I were thrilled. Myles is currently in his fourth year of a five-year program. He pays his tuition balance on his own, and we all expect a bright future for him.

Reflecting on This Miracle

> Now to Him who is able to do exceedingly abundantly above all that we ask or think, according to the power that works in us.
>
> —Ephesians 3:20

Sharon's Reflections

Was this a miracle? I have no doubt it was God who provided for Myles. The Lord used me as I humbled myself before the financial aid director. He saw my need and our faith as we went to the orientation. Knowing our circumstances, we wondered if it was all in vain. But we serve a God that is bigger than our circumstances. He sent forth a miracle because of our faith and obedience to the Holy Spirit. When God speaks, I know I need to listen because there is always a blessing waiting around the corner.

What the Lord has done in Myles' life is confirmation of His anointing on Myles. My son's thoughts on this miracle were simple and straightforward: "I believed in God and

Continued Miracles: Inspiring Testimonials

prayed. God came through for me."

Your Response

God asked Sharon to share her humiliating financial situation with the financial aid director before He performed her miracle. Has God ever asked you to do something humbling or embarrassing? How did you respond?

Never Give Up (Anne)

Forty days after I gave birth to our youngest child, I landed in the hospital with a systemic infection. I almost died. For four years I was in pain after the baby's delivery, and for three years I was in a wheelchair. I could only trust God. We were unable to get help from anyone for my care, so my husband had to quit his job. Our whole life suffered because of this devastating illness. As a result, we lost our children to the state, and we became homeless.

My husband and I were placed in a family shelter. After a few months our children were given back to us, but it didn't last long. The shelter wouldn't keep our family past four months, so we lost our children again. This time we were homeless for almost a year. We lived in a van and showered at the YMCA.

During this time, I prayed, "God, don't You hear me? Don't You care for me? Where are you, God?" God quieted and comforted me, telling me to be content, to stop crying and accept the circumstances in which He had put us. Gradually, I learned to be happy, knowing Jesus as my all in all.

Then suddenly and unbelievably, God heard and answered my prayers. We found a home. Jesus healed my illness, took away my pain, and gave me His peace. Within a few months our kids came home. Praise God. And we all lived happily ever after … for a while.

Reflecting on This Miracle

I can do all things through Christ who strengthens me.

—Philippians 4:13

Anne's Reflections

Press forward in spite of the mountain in front of you. Make it to the top of the mountain with a smile that your past can't erase. It's not a matter of what I lost along the way. It's about the love that has graced my path. It's about Jesus who has carried me through, and in His love I stand today. You can, too.

Your Response

Anne and her husband went through some very trying circumstances, but they didn't give up hope. How would you have responded in these circumstances?

Supernatural Blessings (Moe)

My wife and I woke up early to get ready for a conference we had been looking forward to attending. The keynote speaker at the conference would be an internationally known author, consultant, and lecturer. We were eager to hear this man speak.

As I was getting ready, I sensed the Holy Spirit speaking to me, directing me to write a check for $1,000 and to fill in the memo field with the words "jet fuel." I shared this with my wife, and she asked me why I was marking those words on the check. I told her it was what the Holy Spirit had instructed me to do.

She then asked me where the money was coming from. I said, "From our savings set aside for buying a new house." (At the time we had saved $7,000 toward a home.) "Are you sure about doing this?" my wife asked me.

"Yes," I replied. We went to the conference, which was well attended, and enjoyed the speech. After the speaker finished his message, he mentioned that the Lord had blessed him with a jet he had not purchased. However, he added, when he visits churches, he never charges a speaker fee, and, as a result, he has to pay for his own travel expenses, such as jet fuel. He asked that at least ten attendees give $1,000 each to cover jet fuel—exactly the amount I wrote on the check before going to the meeting. I got up and handed him the check.

A month earlier, we were advised at my job that we weren't going to have raises and bonuses because things weren't going well. Two weeks after I had given the $1,000, I was at work when my supervisor asked me to come into her office immediately. I didn't know what to think.

She told me she had been asked to give me an envelope from one of the company executives. When I got back to my desk, I opened it—and to my surprise, $10,000 was in it!

Two weeks later, a longtime friend of my parents came to visit us. She asked us about our future plans. We said that we were thinking of buying a house but didn't have the funds to move forward. Our friend then gave us $40,000! She told us to pay her back monthly as much as we could without interest. Tearful, excited, and overjoyed, my wife and I agreed to this arrangement, only to be told two weeks later that we didn't have to pay her back.

Reflecting on This Miracle

> But seek first the kingdom of God and His righteousness and all these things shall be added to you.
>
> —Matthew 6:33

> "Bring all the tithes into the storehouse, that there may be meat in My house, and try me now in this," says the Lord of hosts, "If I will not open for you the windows of heaven and pour out for you such a blessing that there will not be room enough to receive it."
>
> —Malachi: 3:10

Moe's Reflections

This type of supernatural blessing can happen to anyone. God has no favorites. If we are obedient to God, He will supply all of our needs and desires according to His riches in glory in Christ Jesus. If we claim to be citizens of the kingdom of God (children of God), then we need to practice God's principles in order to fully experience the kingdom lifestyle.

One of the principles of the kingdom is tithing and free-will offerings. The kingdom is a country, and like any country, we pay taxes. In our earthly countries, our taxes help pay for the infrastructure—roads, bridges, public schools, etc. When we give our kingdom taxes (tithes) in our local churches, it helps pay for electricity, gas, salaries, etc. The investments (offerings) help finance the growth and expansion of the church. So if we claim to be children of God, tithes and offerings should be natural for us. Let us seek the kingdom of God.

Your Response

The word *tithe* means a tenth, in other words, ten percent of your income. *Free-will offerings* are additional gifts, over and above the tithe, that the Lord my lead you to give. Do you follow this practice in your giving?

The Apostle Paul advised, "So let each one give as he purposes in his heart, not grudgingly or of necessity; for God loves a cheerful giver" (2 Corinthians 9:7). Do you give cheerfully or grudgingly?

Truly a Miracle (Donna)

Due to health challenges, I hadn't worked for a few weeks. The office manager informed me that I had used up my vacation and sick leave, and I would not be receiving a check. Not only did I not feel well, but now I didn't have an income.

I called the bank to check my account balance which should have had about a hundred dollars. To my surprise, there was five hundred dollars more in my account. It seemed that the office paid me for one week. I was still short on my rent money, however.

I asked God what I should do. I applied for disability benefits, and my paperwork was faxed to the appropriate government office. At the end of that week, a friend of mine said special intercessory prayers for me at my house. She prayed the following Scripture: "Then shall you prosper, if you take care to fulfill the statutes and judgments with which the Lord charged Moses with concerning Israel. Be strong, and of good courage; do not fear or be dismayed" (1 Chronicles 22:13).

The next day when I went to the mailbox to pick up my mail, I found a government envelope with a one-week disability payment inside. The enclosed government forms stated that the process time would be at least three weeks from receipt of the paperwork. The post office would take another three to five days to deliver my processed disability check. My blessing came in a few days instead of a month. I got down on my knees and thanked God. Through prayers God interceded and answered. I cried for ten minutes.

Reflecting on This Miracle

Get wisdom, get understanding! Do not forget, nor turn away from the words of my mouth.

—Proverbs 4:5

Donna's Reflections

God kept me well for a long time. You must keep faith. Don't always ask God for things. Just ask for guidance. Don't give up. He knows what is best for you. Eventually, He'll show you the way. He's always got a way.

Your Response

How do you respond when you are up against a financial deadline?

6
Forgiveness is the Way

Remember His marvelous works which He has done, His wonders, and the judgments of His mouth.
—1 Chronicles 16:12

Safe in His Dwelling (Samantha)

Duct-taped and wrapped in a gasoline-soaked sheet, my father was trapped in his car which was set on fire. In the aftermath of that horror my mother turned to drugs to cope with the pain. She was no longer able to take care of me. At six-years-old, my security was shattered, sending me into shock. Abandoned, I was left to the responsibility of my grandparents.

Grand-Mom and Grand-Pop took me into their home and totally replaced my parents. They were always there for me, no matter what time of day or night. They showed me lots of love and taught me how to build a relationship with God. Grand-Mom taught me the 23rd Psalm, and Grand-Pop taught me how to pray.

I learned to trust God, and He became my best friend, my safe place, and my comfort. I allowed the joy of the Lord to be my strength. I've learned to forgive my debtors because if I didn't, I knew God would never forgive me. Forgiveness is more than just verbal. It's physical, emotional, spiritual, and mental. I learned this forgiveness lesson at a young age.

The overall outcome has been thankfulness to God for the eternal friendship I gained through the tragedies in my life. Today, I am sixteen-years-old, a positive person with a warm heart and a big smile.

Reflecting on This Miracle

> For in the time of trouble he will keep me safe in his dwelling; He shall hide me in His pavilion, in the secret place of His tabernacle he shall hide me; He shall set me high upon a rock. . . . When my father and mother forsake me, then the Lord will take care
>
> of me.

—Psalm 27:5, 10-11

Samantha's Reflections

Allow the joy of the Lord to become your strength and learn to trust in the Lord with all your heart. And lean not on your own understanding, but in all your ways

Continued Miracles: Inspiring Testimonials

acknowledge Him, and He will direct your path.

Your Response

Would you be able to forgive if this happened to you?

Forgiveness (Sam)

I am the oldest son of a major general in the Sri Lankan Army and an illustrious prep school teacher. I left Sri Lanka in 1985 to study in the United States. My family was Anglican, but as my parents pursued God, they wanted more than the status quo the high church had to offer. They started a church in Krilapone in the late 1970s and were very involved in that ministry.

In May of 1991, I received a phone call that dramatically changed my life. The phone call was from an aunt. She told me that my parents had been murdered—and the person responsible was my youngest brother who was fifteen at the time. He had been living at home with our parents while my other brother, Suresh, was at school in England.

Both Suresh and I traveled immediately to Sri Lanka to attend our parents' funeral. Upon our arrival, we learned that our precious younger brother, whom we both loved deeply, had a fit of rage after being disciplined by our father for cutting classes. When our father told him he could not attend a party with his friends, an argument ensued which ended with the death of both our parents and a batman, or military aide, who had faithfully served my father as a dedicated soldier.

I had grown up in a traditional Christian Sri Lankan family, but now my world as I knew it was dealt a crushing blow with three of the most important people in my life affected by it. A senseless, selfish act cut short the lives of my vibrant, productive, and happy parents.

I spoke a few words at my parents' funeral to a stunned crowd consisting of family, friends, and a community grasping for answers. Nothing anyone could say would bring healing and meaning to this violent and untimely death of God's precious servants. I likened it to the passage in the book of Acts when Steven, full of the Holy Spirit and known for his outstanding work in the ministry, was martyred for his faith. Steven's death was attributed to Saul who acted on his twisted religious convictions.

In spite of the inconsolable grief I felt at the loss of my parents, and the predicament my younger brother had put himself in, I knew God had prepared me for the walk ahead. I came to know the Lord as a teenager while attending college. The faith my parents had demonstrated was further strengthened while I attended Oral Roberts University. I came to know the Lord in a deep and meaningful way and forged my own relationship with Him.

John 10:10 says, "The thief does not come except to steal, and to kill, and to destroy. I am come that they may have life, and have it more abundantly." This verse was about to be tested in my life. In a corn field in Oklahoma, I made a commitment to the Lord that, come what may, I would testify to God's goodness and mercy.

My commitment would be tested time and time again as we started the journey of reconciliation between my younger brother and the Lord, his relatives, his community, and society. We obtained permission from the courts to have our younger brother attend the funeral so he could pay his last respects before the burial.

My brother Suresh and I also visited the military aide's family, apologized, and identified with them over the senseless loss of a loved one. We tried to bring comfort to our parents' siblings and friends, who had many questions about how this could happen in a Christian home. Did our parents have sin in their lives? Had they missed God? Had they missed the signs?

Continued Miracles: Inspiring Testimonials

My brother and I lived out the faith we knew and took courage that the Lord of our parents would also deliver us from evil just as we had prayed time and time again, reciting the Lord's Prayer as youngsters. Suresh and I were confident that the message our parents would leave us from the grave was to take care of our brother and to be part of his reconciliation. "Jesus said to him, 'Let the dead bury their own dead, but you go and preach the Kingdom of God'" (Luke 9:60). We needed to move on and get busy with the task at hand. We knew from our parents' example that "For to me, to live is Christ, and to die is gain" (Philippians 1:21).

Suresh decided to stay behind in Sri Lanka to take care of family matters and act as our younger brother's guardian. He also started to work with the attorneys who were preparing our brother's defense. They crafted an approach of personal responsibility with an appeal for leniency due to our brother's age and the circumstances surrounding this family tragedy. While asking for mercy, we refused to make any attempt to unduly influence the judge or jury.

All of these activities were bathed in prayers that Jehovah-Jireh, our provider, would provide for us, even before we asked—not for riches but for mercy and justice, along with restitution of a young life tied to and robbed by the enemy of our soul.

Not only had we lost our loving parents, but a divided Sri Lanka had lost Tamil role models. Our parents lived and worked as Christians first and Sri Lankans second to bring understanding and reconciliation to a society where communal hatred and intolerance boiled over in 1983 and beyond.

I am happy to report to you that, twenty years later, in spite of setbacks along the way, my younger brother is a free man, having served out his sentence and parole. Suresh and I have forgiven him for his selfish and senseless act and continue to commit ourselves to bringing healing and restoration to our brother. We thank God for our pastors and other Christian leaders who came alongside us to provide loving accountability and resources needed for the road ahead.

Reflecting on This Miracle

> The wicked is banished in his wickedness, but the righteous has a refuge in His death.
> — Proverbs 14:32
>
> If anyone serves Me, let him follow Me; and where I am, there my servant will also be. If anyone serves me, My father will honor him.

— John 12:26

Your glorifying is not good. Do you not know that a little leaven leavens the whole lump?

— 1 Corinthians 5:6

For I am hard-pressed between the two having a desire to depart and be with Christ, which is far better.

—Philippians 1:23

Sam's Reflections

It is our prayer to see our brother fulfill God's call on his life (a task God gives someone to do). I believe, according to Ephesians 2:10, as Pastor Dishan preached on missions Sunday, "Workmanship not only includes our talents, gifts, abilities and past performance, but our past failures, weaknesses and shortcomings woven together by a loving God, who has gone before us and prepared a life for us now, not only in the next life, so we can fulfill His plan for our lives."

One can wonder, did that anchor hold these twenty years during the vicious and violent tsunamis of life? I am here to tell you yes, it did, as we anchored ourselves on the rock of Jesus. He has not only given us preserving grace and mercy, but strength and love to bring restoration to our brother.

Continued Miracles: Inspiring Testimonials

Your Response

Would you be able to forgive if you were Sam? Is there someone you need to forgive now?

Continued Miracles: Inspiring Testimonials

7

Divinely Healed for a Purpose

He does miracles when we need them—not for our entertainment or to make us feel "spiritual."
— Craig S. Keener

Answered Prayer for May (May)

I was in for a surprise.

Snow fell outside one cold evening as I watched through our living room window. The lights were off. I had just arrived home from the hospital where my husband, Joe, was near death. Concerned, I prayed to the Lord at the hospital, on the way home, and on arriving home.

I asked God to show me a sign that Joe would be alright. An angel of the Lord appeared down the hallway. She was so beautiful and stood on a cloud about a foot off the ground. Her long gold hair and gold dress sparkled like stars and moved off to the side in a wind. Her feet were very small, and I could see pink toes peeking out of the cloud. Her large, pure-white wings stood about a foot above her head and flapped gently. They sounded like leaves rustling in the wind. I said, "My, oh my. You are so beautiful." Then I asked the angel, "Does this mean Joe's going to be okay? God's not taking him now, is He?" I could feel the angel's smile which reassured me. "This is so wonderful."

I watched as the angel glided into the living room. She came around me on her right side, stood in front of me, and leaned forward. Smiling, she placed her hands on my shoulders and arms, producing a warmth where her hands touched. I did not see her face. Then the angel backed up down the hall and disappeared. I fell into a peaceful sleep, and I didn't wake up until eight o'clock in the morning. I thought, "This blanket feels so warm." But when I looked down, I realized there was no blanket over me. The angel had placed a "blanket of prayers" on me. God had given me peace.

The Holy Spirit then softly spoke to me: "You have seen a miracle. I would like you to tell everyone who will listen what you have seen." I exclaimed, "I promise. I promise. I will. I will." I believe this was a miracle from God. I still get excited sharing the miracle with everyone, and it is a blessing that Joe has lived over ten years since then. I am grateful for my touch from the Lord.

Continued Miracles: Inspiring Testimonials

Reflecting on This Miracle

> Ask and it will be given you; Seek and you will find; Knock and it will be opened to you. For everyone who asks receives, he who seeks finds, and to him who knocks, it will be opened.
>
> —Matthew 7:7, 8

May's Reflections

I fervently sought the Lord on my husband's behalf since he was not able to pray for himself. I did not cease in my prayers and believed that God would answer them. You have to believe. Have faith in your heart as well as your mouth. If the Holy Spirit speaks to you, don't get scared and run. Listen. If you don't believe, you may not receive.

Your Response

Do you pray to God for help when you or someone you know is ill, in an accident, or in an emergency? Do you pray every day?

An Unexpected Recovery (Carolyn)

I had a hysterectomy years ago around Mother's Day, and while most women want to forget this surgery, I have a special reason for remembering mine.

That Mother's Day would be different. I prayed before surgery and just prior to undergoing anesthesia. My church friends prayed, too. Usually after this type of surgery, it takes a day for the anesthesia to wear off, but I didn't recover from anesthesia for two days. On Thursday, I thought it was Tuesday.

Once I was coherent, my doctor informed me that complications occurred as a result of the surgery, and I might have nerve damage in my left leg for the rest of my life. My left leg kept collapsing under me when I put weight on it. I needed a cane for balance and stability.

A week after my discharge from the hospital, I took a shower, and I sensed God prompting me to turn off the cold water and let the hot water hit my left leg. My husband came in the bathroom because he heard mumbling, and he found me in the shower with only the hot water running. He thought I would scald my leg. Two days later, my left leg began to recover. I had less numbness and more strength. My prayers for the healing of my leg were answered.

A week later I went to the doctor for a follow-up appointment, and he was excited to learn that my left leg was healed. It was by the stripes of Jesus that I was healed. The doctor was amazed. I was even able to return to my job as a certified nurse's aide.

Reflecting on This Miracle

O Lord my God, I cried to You, and You healed me.

—Psalm 30:2

Carolyn's Reflections

This experience has brought me even closer to God and given me the incentive to share with others. Only God knows what would have happened if I had not been healed. I thank God every day for Jesus shedding his blood on the cross and for the knowledge that He gave His life to save us. I wish everyone could know and believe in Him.

Your Response

Do you pray prior to surgery? What would your attitude be toward God if you prayed and your surgery didn't turn out as you expected?

Cloud Burst (Debbie)

Dark clouds loomed overhead on Sunday morning; the rain was coming.

My friend Heidi had invited me to her church, and she told me the church van would pick me up. Since our street was hard to find, I decided to wait at the intersection to make it easier for the driver, but it was getting later and later, and the van had not arrived.

Continued Miracles: Inspiring Testimonials

Another friend, Cheri, was driving by when she saw me standing at the corner, and she stopped to inquire why I was standing there. Before she drove off, she said, "If the van doesn't come soon, I'll drive you to church." After more waiting I knew the service would start in ten minutes so I opted to take Cheri's offer. We drove to the church with dark clouds chasing us, and we arrived on time. I was glad to find my friend waiting with a smile, and we got settled for the service which started promptly.

A visiting pastor from North Carolina was speaking. He had a unique style of presenting live demonstrations and real-life examples from the Word. Partway through the service, he sauntered across the sanctuary with the Bible in his hands and stopped suddenly. He said, "If anyone in here has a stomach issue and can't eat certain foods, stand up."

I shot up like a thunderbolt. God called me out in front of the whole congregation and spoke to me through the pastor. I glanced around and realized that no one else was standing around me.

When I turned toward the pastor, he declared, "You are healed in the name of Jesus Christ"! My mouth dropped open as the Word struck me like a lightning bolt. I believed I was released from irritable bowel syndrome which had persisted for nearly fifty years and from a more recent diagnosis, celiac disease. I believed what I heard, that my suffering was over, and I felt relieved. Praise God!

I reluctantly recalled how I came to be diagnosed with celiac disease. A few years before, my dog Juno and I had narrowly escaped a house fire on a bitter cold day, two weeks before Christmas. I sat with Juno in the back of a police squad car in shock and with the flames of the house still raging. The smell of the smoke repulsed me, and I couldn't go back inside to get anything. I felt like an animal caught in a trap. I had only my cell phone (without its charger), the purple stadium coat on my back, and Juno. My poor dog was confused and disoriented.

I was distraught; I had to be relocated miles away that afternoon, and by evening my cell phone had died. My heart sank even further when Juno bolted out the open door into the nearby woods after I returned from the convenience store.

Have you ever tried to find a white dog in the dark with snow falling? I kept praying out loud and crying out to God through this ordeal. Thankfully, Juno and I were reunited later after I yelled "treat" and dangled in the air a piece of bread, given to me by an unknown neighbor. When Juno finally appeared, looking bedraggled from his stressful jaunt through the woods, he grabbed the treat, and I snagged him by the collar, dragging him back.

I was blessed to get a cell phone charger and a few other necessities, so that life started to return to something near normality. I continued working and persevering, but then the digestive problems began. I wanted to eat, and yet I didn't want to eat. For two weeks I couldn't keep food down. My stomach ached, and I imagined it resembled a crater inside. I didn't want to venture outside with my stomach not feeling well, knowing it could cause a problem at any time. I had no strength, and my clothes hung on my bones.

At the doctor's office the nurse wanted me to get on the scale which was usually a non-threatening procedure, but I hesitated to comply. When I finally stood on the scale, I was stunned to find that my weight had dropped to eighty eight pounds. I was near death.

A gluten-free baker I had met suggested I get tested for celiac disease. When I suggested this to my doctors, they agreed. My allergist scheduled a blood test, and my internist ordered an endoscopy. The results came back positive.

I didn't like taking on a new label, but I knew God was going to bring me through this. I reluctantly eliminated wheat, barley, rye and oats from my diet and voraciously read twenty books in two months on the subject. In the meantime, I reasoned that if God performed miracles in the Bible, He could do the same for me. I prayed, declared my healing daily, and quoted out loud healing Scriptures from the Bible.

My trip down memory lane was interrupted when the pastor said, "Whoever has a heart issue, stand up." I continued standing in anticipation because I remembered how I had gone for testing on my heart which raced continually after the fire trauma. A well-qualified cardiologist had gently but firmly informed me that the test results indicated I needed
surgery.

"Who, me?" I had responded. "At my age?" This diagnosis had been a shock because I walked frequently, and I thought I was in pretty good shape. I had paused for a minute, looked at the doctor, and declared, "I'll be back when I have a miracle." I thanked the doctor, picked up my purse, paid the receptionist, and went home without medication or a surgery date, huffing, "God's got my back"! My faith had to carry me through.

Now, eight months later, as I stood in front of this congregation, the visiting pastor declared, "You are healed in the name of Jesus Christ"! I was amazed at the Lord.

Continued Miracles: Inspiring Testimonials

My church suggested I repeat the testing, and I beamed when the doctor wrote, "No surgery required" on my chart. Elated, I ran down the hall of the hospital, claiming God's blessing.

I wasn't a strong believer for many years, so I wouldn't have envisioned a miracle. Thankfully, God changed my life as I watched and waited for my miracle. I stood in faith that God would bring a miracle, but I didn't know when or where.

There wasn't an awe-inspired buzz in this service when the pastor declared my miracles as in Bible times when someone was healed. Jesus performed "visible" miracles centuries ago, and His fame spread throughout the regions. Since the people in that church couldn't see inside my stomach or heart, I don't think they understood the impact of the pastor's words.

Overwhelmed, I went home and cried for two hours. God spared my life. Hallelujah, I am now set free from both diagnoses.

Reflecting on This Miracle

This is the day the Lord has made; we will be glad and rejoice in it.

—Psalm 118:24

Continued Miracles: Inspiring Testimonials

Debbie's Response

Press your way through when you think you may back out of an opportunity. If the rain had come while I was waiting for the van or if I didn't get a ride, I might have backed out of attending the service and missed the blessing of these two miracles.

Your Response

Would you be able to trust God enough to leave a doctor's office without treatment?

Do you believe a miracle is still possible after many years?

Epileptic Healing (Luz)

Beginning at twelve-years-old, I suffered from daily epileptic seizures for twenty years. During these episodes, which happened without warning, I lost control of everything. I was given strong, daily medications to treat the seizures, but they provided minimal success. The doctors told my parents that I might never have a normal life with marriage and children.

One day at my church, the pastor called me to the altar and said, "Today is your healing." In awe, I was instantly healed. Gone were the days of anxiety and embarrassment from the unpredictability of my seizures and lack of control. I was free of seizures, medications, and doctor visits.

I did marry, and now I have a son, a granddaughter, and a grandson who are all healthy. After having epilepsy for twenty years, it is my joy to continually tell about my instant healing. Only Jesus could do such a miracle. Praise the Lord for my healing.

Reflecting on This Miracle

> But He said, "The things which are impossible with men are possible with God."
>
> —Luke 18:27

Luz's Reflections

Be a persistent believer, so that you will receive the healing.

Your Response

Do you believe you can be healed in an instant?

God's Will (Lerma)

At my three-month maternity check-up, I was informed that, because I was thirty-five-years-old, the baby was at high risk with a sixty-percent chance for Downs Syndrome. The doctors advised me to abort the baby, but I believed God had given me this child, so I refused. The senior physician said I should go for counseling, and he made an appointment for me.

My husband and I were on our way to the appointment (for measurement of the baby and for counseling) when I remembered that I hadn't eaten breakfast. We stopped at a restaurant across from the doctor's office, and after discussing the situation, we decided that I didn't need to go to the appointment, so we went back home.

The head of the gynecology office called later about the missed appointment, insisted that I really needed to get counseling, and made another appointment for me. This time I went to the appointment. I was examined and a report was sent to my gynecologist. At my subsequent exam the doctor did not tell me the results. I was only told that I had to get still another test in which they would draw fluid from the placenta. They claimed it was a routine procedure, but I said, "Oh, no—I'm not doing that."

At my next checkup they said I had diabetes, and they had me drink a solution containing sugar. This procedure was repeated at another checkup. And yet, despite the diabetic scare, my pregnancy was going well; I was doing alright.

Before the baby came, I had a dream in which I was holding a healthy baby. I remembered that, in the dream, the baby was a boy, but he looked like a girl.

The doctor had to do an emergency Caesarean, but our baby boy arrived safely, weighing in at 9.7 pounds. He was fine with no sign of Down's syndrome. Today, he is a healthy toddler, running around and having fun. And, yes, his hair does make him look like a girl—just like in the dream.

Reflecting on This Miracle

> Now faith is the substance of things hoped for, the evidence of things not seen.
> —Hebrews 11:1

Lerma's Reflections

If God has promised you something, then stand on God's promise even when nothing looks good. This is a test of your faith.

Your Response

What would have been your response in this situation?

Continued Miracles: Inspiring Testimonials

Would you have listened to the doctors or to God's promise?

I'm Not Ready (Fran)

I was the fourth runner-up for the Mrs. New Jersey Senior America Pageant, held in Atlantic City in 2003. Makeup and fashion have always been an integral part of my lifestyle. Does it surprise you, then, to hear that over thirty years before, I once left the house without any makeup? That was one day that I wouldn't miss makeup— after all, I was headed for the hospital . . . near death.

In 1972 I had a lot of pain in my stomach for several days, and I had no idea why. With my husband at my side, I went to the emergency room. X-rays were ordered for me, and even though I was very weak, I asked to see them. I was a practicing X-ray technician for years, and I knew good images from bad ones. My X-rays looked like black smoke, which indicated immediate danger.

I was prepped for an emergency operation. The surgeons did not know what the problem was, what to expect, or what the chances for my survival might be. My husband, wondering if I would ever see him or our daughter again, begged the surgeons to save my life, and he asked a priest to perform last rites. I had been praying at home and at the hospital that, if it were the Lord's will, I might live. I wasn't ready to be with the Lord just yet.

The surgery was successful, and I survived. It was discovered that I had had an obstruction and issues from a previous surgery. The surgeons said that I must be a good person or have led a good life because they thought I was going to die of complications on the operating table. The principal of the school, where our daughter attended, made a special visit to the hospital to encourage me that the whole school and church were praying for me.

Today, I organize retreats for our church and take care of my family. I still wear makeup almost every day. I have been a beauty consultant for over twenty years, helping women improve their images.

Reflecting on This Miracle
> Jesus said to him, "If you can believe, all things are possible to him who believes."
>
> —Mark 9:23

Fran's Response

I pray for others all the time, but I never thought that I would end up near death, praying for my own survival, but God had a purpose for me. I am still alive. Believe in the

Lord and have strong faith, regardless of your situation or diagnosis. Cling to hope.

Your Response

Have you ever prayed before major surgery or had a church congregation praying for you? Do you believe that prayer can change your circumstances? What can you do to take yourself to the next level of faith in the Lord?

Love Conquers All (Lori)

When I was first diagnosed with breast cancer, my doctor said it was caught early, but since it was a fast growing type, I needed surgery in three weeks. On the drive home from the doctor's office after receiving the news, we pulled into a parking lot. As the alarm and fear of the diagnosis began to register with me, I sat in that parking lot and dissolved in tears. "Why me?" I cried. Five years before, I watched my father die. Now I was afraid I was going to be next. My mammogram two years previous had shown a shadow which was alarming. It eventually turned out to be nothing, but it scared me so much that I didn't that I didn't have another mammogram the following year. Now, I was being confronted with this dreaded diagnosis and faced with the upcoming surgery.

Continued Miracles: Inspiring Testimonials

I had never had surgery before, and I didn't want to be put to sleep for fear of not waking up. My major concern was what my family would do without me. My anger with God about my diagnosis prevented me from praying before the surgery. Despite that, my first surgery, a lumpectomy, went well. I was thankful for the love and support of Wayne, my daughter Stacy, and my granddaughter Lorna.

Wayne consistently prayed for me during and after that operation and the three ensuing surgeries I had over the next two years. He gave me strength, love, and courage. Though I was angry with God and wouldn't pray, each time I woke up from surgery, I said, "Thank you, God."

My second surgery also went well, but I was terrified of the chemotherapy treatments that were to follow. I even delayed chemotherapy for a month so I could be sure I wasn't too ill to enjoy an upcoming Paul McCartney concert which Wayne and I were eagerly anticipating. After the concert, I felt happy and contented— it was just what I needed to get me through the ordeal. It also helped that I have a good sense of humor which has carried me through the darkest of times. It's hard to be depressed and humorous at the same time.

A pump for the chemo delivery, called a portocath, was installed, and I began my rounds of treatment. Hair loss was a side effect of the chemotherapy along with nausea and weariness. I scouted around for a look-alike wig to boost my self-esteem. I wore a lot of colorful hats and scarves as well which made me feel better. I was at peace with myself, knowing I had done my best to walk this path, and I was improving.

However, after enduring four rounds of chemo and thirty-six rounds of radiation within a year, my attitude changed, I felt worthless and wondered why I was going through such difficulties. Sharing love and humor with others is what brought me through this ordeal. Today, when I have a mammogram, I sometimes flash back to my cancer diagnosis and become afraid, but this is typical of any cancer survivor. Deep down I know everything will be alright. Every year I am cancer-free, I shout, "Hallelujah, He saved me again"! Miracles are answers to prayer.

Anxiety attacks and elevated blood pressure occurred routinely after my surgeries, partly from my struggle with cancer and partly from the stress of taking care of my aging mother. I did the best I could, but I eventually realized that my mother needed the more extensive care of an assisted living facility.

As I started praying more consistently with Wayne, my anxiety diminished, and my blood pressure came down.

With Stacy's help, I started a local team for the annual breast cancer walk. I was able to whiz around the lake trail in my wheelchair with my family pushing me in turns. Now that I am healed, Stacy and I continue to attend breast cancer walks and to stand with others who are still battling this disease. Lorna, my teenage granddaughter, also pours out her love to me and others with cancer.

I have been cancer-free for over five years, and I am very active. I continue to walk each week and swim twelve laps a day. I ride my scooter while walking our dog. Spending time with Wayne makes me glad to be alive.

Reflecting on This Miracle

> Let us make every effort to do what leads to peace and mutual edification.
>
> —Romans 14:9 (NIV)

Lori's Reflections

My spiritual walk grows daily as I continue to have hope, stay faithful, be grateful, and love others. Wayne and I now study the Bible and pray together every day. I like the Serenity Prayer best.

Your Response

Lori trusted God, but she admitted to being afraid as well. Do you think it's possible to have faith but still experience doubts and fears?

Loving the Lord Through it All (Tina)

I am a daughter of the living King, Jesus. I am not self-sufficient but God-sufficient. I am also a paraplegic. As a people person and an encourager, I have a zeal for sharing the gospel through the leading of the Holy Spirit wherever He may guide me. Involved with my church, and especially with anyone seeking or searching for the true meaning of life, I long to allow the Lord to use me as vessel (a person set aside for God's use in bringing glory to Him). But this wasn't always the way I lived.

I've been a paraplegic for twenty-three years, and I have endured many challenges—not only physical but also emotional. I've lost my dog, my brother, and, when my husband left me, my marriage. But none of it stopped my drive and enthusiasm for the Lord.

I loved my dog, Choco, a golden retriever/Irish setter mix with dark brown eyes. We were inseparable best friends for years. It was hard to let him go because he gave me unconditional love and comfort.

Continued Miracles: Inspiring Testimonials

While recovering from the loss of Choco, I was blindsided when my brother took his own life. This sent me reeling, and I thought my world was crashing down around me. But God gave me peace in the knowledge that my brother had given his life to Jesus ten months before. After he was saved, all he talked about was God's mercy.

My brother's death made me realize that something was missing in my life because, before his passing, I had no relationship with Jesus. My brother had given me a Bible for Christmas, and after his death, in God's great timing, I opened the Bible, and the Holy Spirit opened my eyes. My life changed for the better through this tragedy. I learned that all things work together for good for those who love God, just as it says in Romans 8:28.

A new dilemma surfaced when I started losing strength in my left arm. Doctors thought that I had developed a cyst in my neck, so an MRI was performed. Based on the results, three different doctors told me I needed surgery to have a stent placed in my neck, or my arms would be paralyzed in a month.

I dreaded the possibility of more surgery, but while relaxing over a cup of tea, this thought kept running through my head: "You're going to be OK. Just trust Me."

Continued Miracles: Inspiring Testimonials

I asked, "Lord, trust You? How can this be? Are You speaking to me? Please make it more clear to me."

Then I heard from the Holy Spirit, "Just trust me. You won't need surgery. You will be healed. When you go to the fourth doctor on Monday, you will hear something different."

I responded, "Lord, forgive me for my unbelief because I don't believe what I think I'm hearing. Lord, if this is where You want me, please help me to accept it."

On Monday I went to see a neurologist who reviewed my MRI and then asked, "Why are you here?" I explained my diagnosis. He replied, "Well, you do have a syrinx (a fluid-filled cavity in the spinal cord), and it's pressing on the nerves in your spinal cord. You can have surgery which you may not survive, or you can live with the strong possibility of a stroke or paralysis of your arms. I do not want to see your arms like your legs. Can you live with this?"

I replied, "Absolutely."

"I say we wait, do another MRI, and keep an eye on your situation," the doctor concluded.

Continued Miracles: Inspiring Testimonials

Emotionally torn, I turned to the Lord again: "Lord, if you will only give me six more months with use of my arms . . ." It was hard to fathom giving up anything else. I wanted to keep the freedom my arms allowed.

After two months of lying in bed with throbbing neck pain, I looked to Him. "Lord, I can't take it anymore. I want to be healed. Lord, forgive me. Help me be patient. I want what you want." Tears streamed down my face like a waterfall.

The next morning when I woke up, I was pain-free, and I didn't need to take my pain medication. Hallelujah! I was overjoyed—what a miracle! "Thank you, Jesus," I declared. "I'm healed"! I didn't need to have the surgery. A year later at a check-up, I learned I had thirteen bead-like cysts. The surgery would have required thirteen stents instead of one—a medical impossibility.

Reflecting on This Miracle

> Fear not, for I am with you; be not dismayed, for I am your God. I will strengthen you, yes, I will help you, I will uphold you with My righteous right hand.
>
> —Isaiah 41:10

Continued Miracles: Inspiring Testimonials

But Jesus looked at them and said to them, "With men this is impossible, but with God all things are possible."

—Mark 19:26

Tina's Reflections

At one point through my health issues, I thought I should jump ship because I saw myself in a nursing home unable to move. I recall satan trying to tell me I would lose the use of my arms. I thought I was alone in all this. I called out, "Lord, no one on earth can help me but You." He comforted me. It's been over ten years since I was diagnosed, and God remained faithful. I am thankful He gave me salvation and a miraculous healing. He doesn't owe me anything, but He gives me everything useful for His kingdom. He can do the same for you.

Your Response

Would you be able to trust the Lord's promise that you would be alright like Tina did?

Radical Faith (Lisa)

I first noticed my physical change when I tried to put on my eyeliner, and I couldn't keep the brush in my hand from shaking. I would call my friend to come over and put on my eyebrows, and we both had a good laugh.

But then the problems escalated. When I dropped something on the floor and bent over to get it, I strained to stand back up. In fact, once when I crouched down to put air in my car tire, my knees were so weak that I could not rise again.

When I called my doctor for an appointment, I was told that she was out of the office for a month's vacation, so I agreed to be seen by a nurse practitioner. After examining me, the practitioner said, "I think this is stress related. I'm prescribing an antidepressant."

"No, I don't do drugs, and I am not depressed," I replied and stormed out of the office without the prescription. Something was going on with my body, and no one believed me. The nurse called me at home, insisting that I return to the office and get the prescription. I told her to stop calling me, and I vowed to never return to that office again.

A month went by, and I began to have difficulty swallowing and excessive sweating as if I were doing a workout. My initial symptoms grew worse and the shaking progressed. I couldn't keep food in my stomach for longer than fifteen or twenty minutes. It took several glasses of water to swallow just a few bites, so I stopped eating, and my weight dropped.

The next month I stopped at a light while driving to work, and my car was hit from behind. I was taken by ambulance to the hospital with a neck injury and excruciating pain. After taking X-rays of my neck, the ER physician told me I needed to go immediately to my primary hospital. He insisted it was an emergency.

I was transferred to my primary hospital where a surgeon ordered additional X-rays and a battery of tests. After evaluating the results, the surgeon walked into my hospital room with a look of concern and said, "You have stage-two thyroid cancer; we're starting radiation therapy tonight. If you survive this, you will never be able to speak above a whisper."

This diagnosis was unbelievable, but somehow I knew I wouldn't die. Angry, I decided to treat this condition as just an inconvenience, nothing more than a temporary moment in my very full life. I didn't have time for illness.

I continued to work every week, but the cancer depleted my energy, and doing simple things made me feel as if I had run a marathon. Although I still attended church,

I didn't ask anyone at church to pray for me, and I didn't pray any more than usual. The Bible says that God answers my prayers, so I didn't need others to pray for me. It is my opinion that you either believe the Word or you don't.

My doctors placed me on a strict diet of liquids only, and I followed a radiation regimen twice each week. I was angry that the radiation took my hair out, removed my eyebrows and eyelashes, and changed the texture of my skin.

Surgery was scheduled to remove the malignant growth which had become as large as a football and hung from the base of my tongue down to my chest, putting pressure on my heart. I was told that my heart could stop at any time. As the tumor rapidly grew larger, it wrapped itself around my vocal cords. My surgeon had performed a procedure, like the one I required, only once before, and the tumor in that operation was only the size of a golf ball.

I was relieved when the eight-hour thyroidectomy was successful. After the surgery I was so hungry that I begged my dad to get me some broccoli. I wanted to taste real food again. My first bite tasted so good! But when I tried to swallow, it was like swallowing glass. Needless to say, I went back to the liquids—water, ice, ice cream, and jello.

Since then, I have made a full recovery, and I am overjoyed to have my inconvenient illness behind me. I enjoy being with family and friends and working at my job. I love to sing, and the surgery has not impaired my voice— I even joined the church choir.

Reflecting on This Miracle

> Now faith is the substance of things hoped for, the evidence of things not seen.
>
> —Hebrews 11:1

Lisa's Reflections

Have that blind faith you've heard about, don't let it waver, and God will bring you through. All you need is faith the size of a mustard seed.

Your Response

What would you do if you were Lisa? Would you treat cancer as an "inconvenience" rather than a disease?

Waiting Patiently (Michelle)

God told my husband that we would have a promised son, just as Abraham and Sarah in the Bible were promised a son from God. This was a test of faith, and we waited patiently. When I became pregnant, we thought our blessing was on the way. But then I had a miscarriage, followed by a second one within six months. Although we were disheartened, we kept the faith and trusted God.

We finally received our long- awaited blessing, a promised son. Today he is a smiling, playful toddler, running all over the house. God was faithful, and He delivered what He promised.

Reflecting on This Miracle

> Trust in the Lord with all your heart, and lean not to your own understanding.
>
> —Proverbs 3:5

Michelle's Reflections

Intimacy with God builds expectation which becomes the breeding ground for miracles. You must be in relationship with God, knowing Him personally and having a tangible, real experience with Him.

Your Response

If you were in this situation, would you continue to trust God for a son, even after two miscarriages? Would you still trust God in the face of a detour or a long delay?

Continued Miracles: Inspiring Testimonials

8

God Works Through Animals

Never lose hope because, although miracles are rare, they are possible.
— Anonymous

Bailey the Yorkie (Sandy)

When I rescued Bailey, a teacup Yorkie, from illegal breeders, he weighed three pounds, two ounces at nine months-old. He was all fur and bones. I couldn't get him to eat, and he cried continually for the first year I had him. I wanted to take him for walks, but Bailey was physically unable to walk. Even with all the extra tender loving care we gave him, my friends were afraid he would die and leave me heartbroken.

While Bailey was at the veterinarians for a routine procedure, I learned that his blood results were high, indicating liver failure. The vet hesitated to tell me because he knew it would upset me. "I can't believe it," I said. "I just rescued this dog. Why should I put him through any more surgery?" The vet responded, "Have a little faith. I don't want anything to happen to this pup. Whether he lives six months or six years, he's going to have a better life with you than the life he would have had where he came from. Take him home and enjoy him."

One day, shortly after Bailey had been diagnosed with liver disease, I met another woman, Debbie, walking her dog Juno in front of my house. We began talking, and I shared Bailey's story with her. She encouraged me to pray and to believe that Bailey would be alright. She promised to intercede for Bailey too.

By Christmas Bailey's appetite had picked up, and he was more active and playful. It made me smile just to look at him. I took Bailey back to the vet who originally examined him, and the vet noticed a significant change. "Little boy," he said, "you are getting buffed. You now have muscle." Bailey had grown an inch and gained a pound.

Bailey had more blood work, and this time the results were good—no more liver disease. My prayers had been answered! I got down on my knees, cried, and thanked God. This was the best Christmas present I ever received. Bailey is now a playful four-year-old, weighing in at six pounds. If you saw Bailey now, you would never think he had been so sick.

Reflecting on This Miracle

> For the word of the Lord is right, and all His work is done in truth.
>
> —Psalm 33:4

Sandy's Reflections

People should believe in God and have faith. Prayer never fails.

Your Response

Would you have the faith to pray for the health of a dog? Do you think God is concerned about such things as the health of our pets?

Bella

When the Philadelphia Phillies won the 2008 World Series, Philadelphia exploded in joy. The area was electric; spontaneous parties popped up everywhere; celebratory fireworks were set off.

Meanwhile, Bella, a six-month-old, copper-colored pup about the size of a small Chihuahua or toy poodle, was out for her evening walk. When the fireworks went off, so did Bella. She was so scared she slipped out of her harness and took off on an unknown journey. Her owners were devastated and looked everywhere for her, to no avail. While there were many tears of joy that night for the Phillies, tears of sadness were shed for Bella.

The next evening my neighbor called me and said that a man who lived in the complex behind us was searching for his lost puppy. Shortly thereafter, I noticed a young man walking by our apartment, and he looked upset, so I asked him if he had lost a puppy, and he told me about Bella. "We've been looking everywhere for her since last night," he said.

We exchanged phone numbers, and he gave me a poster with his puppy's photo and contact information. Tears streamed down my face as I told him to stay hopeful.
I shared a couple of reassuring stories about retrieving my own dog after he became lost. I also told him that I would pray, that I believed in miracles, and that I believed baby Bella would be found.

While walking my own dog, I searched and called out, "Bella, Bella," hoping she would come. Our neighbors, who were pet owners, searched for her too. I contacted a prayer group about it, and one of the group's members assured me confidently that Bella would be found in a couple of days. I called the owner on his cell phone to give him hope.

Continued Miracles: Inspiring Testimonials

It did seem like a lost cause, though. Our area was well-developed, just twenty minutes from Philadelphia. There were hundreds of stores, highways, traffic galore, and crazed Philly fans. Where did Bella go? Was she in the woods? Was she hit by a car? Only God knew where she was. I was convinced she was in a fight for her life, and I continued praying.

Two days later, a Friday, the celebrations continued. At one o'clock in the afternoon with the sun shining, the Phillies had their first parade in twenty-eight years down Broad Street. Fans checked out of work in record numbers. The stadium was packed as well as the streets.

I was walking to work when my cell phone rang. It was one of Bella's owners—their puppy had been found by three women at a party supply store which was miles away. Amazingly, little Bella had crossed major highways and traveled through wooded areas for two days without food, and she wasn't hurt or killed.

Reflecting on This Miracle

Trust in the Lord with all your heart, and lean not on your own understanding.

—Proverbs 3:5

Continued Miracles: Inspiring Testimonials

> I will seek what was lost and bring back what was driven away, bind up the broken and strengthen what was sick.
>
> —Ezekiel 34:16

Bella's Owners' Reflections

Our faith was stretched and strengthened during this emergency. Have hope.

Your Response

Have you ever lost a pet? Did you reach out to God or try to handle the situation by yourself?

Schatzi (Basia)

The main focus and favorite pastime of our three year old Rottweiler, Schatzi, was eating. Her second favorite pastime was exploring and romping in the backyard with our other dog, Zeus. But something was terribly wrong now: Schatzi hadn't eaten in fourteen days.

I looked all over our fenced-in backyard to make sure there wasn't anything outside she might have eaten, but it looked the same as usual. I took Schatzi to her veterinarian and then to a pet ultrasound facility. When the ultrasound came back negative, the vets were puzzled. She was taken farther away to another veterinary facility for further testing.

Continued Miracles: Inspiring Testimonials

We paid over a thousand dollars for tests and procedures with no diagnosis.

Our family and friends prayed for Schatzi continually. We didn't want to lose her; she was an integral part of our family. We gave her filtered water to keep her from becoming dehydrated. She wasn't moaning, incapacitated, or sleeping longer than usual, so we still clung to hope and watched her closely. God was taking care of her.

Finally, Schatzi passed a large piece of bark and then a walnut. Her new snack had nearly killed her. Almost immediately after being freed from her obstruction, Schatzi was back to her normal self. God saved her. Schatzi doesn't have any ill effects from her incident. She isn't on a special diet, and she doesn't need any care for her stomach. She still loves to eat and play in the yard with our other dog.

Reflecting on This Miracle

Rejoice and exalt in hope, be steadfast and patient suffering and tribulation; be constant in prayer.
—Romans 12:12

Wait on the Lord: be of good courage, and He shall strengthen your heart; wait, I say on the Lord.
—Psalm 27:14

Continued Miracles: Inspiring Testimonials

Basia's Reflections

Try to be patient and let God take His time. There is a point at which you have to stop trying to figure things out. Let God do His work. We don't have all the answers in our heads.

Your Response

What would you do in this situation if you didn't have the money for tests?

The Easter Miracle (Anna)

Fluffy is a long-haired, charcoal-and-white cat with a big, fluffy tail. The faintest bit of white is on the tip of her tail as if it had been dipped in a can of paint. Fluffy's mother showed up for a meal one day at our house with her adorable little kitten. One day Mama disappeared, leaving Fluffy with us. Ten years later and two weeks before Easter, Fluffy wasn't eating or drinking. The veterinarian said Fluffy was in kidney failure and should be put down so she wouldn't have a painful death.

I was upset and couldn't make the decision to let go of my companion of ten years. It was just too difficult. A neighbor suggested another veterinarian who came to the house and gave Fluffy antibiotics, but he wasn't hopeful either. My daughter, Nancy, gave Fluffy the medication four times a day and water from a dropper every hour around the clock. Fluffy still couldn't eat. I prayed, "God, please let me keep my beloved cat."

We prayed all week for Fluffy. I began to lose hope, but my daughter didn't. "Jesus raised Lazarus from the dead. Maybe He'll do the same for Fluffy," Nancy told me, putting her arm around me. "Maybe we'll still have an Easter miracle, Mom. Please don't be so doubtful. God is always giving us small miracles. We just need to recognize them."

I said I was very skeptical of miracles because I had never witnessed any, but Nancy disagreed with me. "If God answers prayers, don't ever tell me you've never seen a miracle."

I finally settled for a compromise. "If Fluffy is better by Easter," I said, "I will go to church Easter Sunday with you and give thanks."

Easter morning, we were eating breakfast when Fluffy got up from her cat bed and ever so slowly made her way to her food dish. To our surprise, she ate everything. Then Fluffy looked at me and gave a faint meow. Crying tears of joy, I got ready to go to church to give thanks to

God, just as I'd promised Nancy. When we went back to our vet, he couldn't detect anything wrong with Fluffy, and he happily said, "Fluffy is back."

Reflecting on This Miracle

> Six days before the Passover, Jesus came to Bethany, where Lazarus lived, whom Jesus raised from the dead.
>
> —John12:1 (NIV)

> . . . and who through the spirit of Holiness was appointed the Son of God in power by his resurrection from the dead: Jesus Christ is Lord.
>
> —Romans 1:4 (NIV)

Nancy's Reflections

Never, never give up hope, whether it's for your pet, husband, wife, or child. We believe our prayers were answered that day. God gave man the ability to create medicine, but only God has the ability to give a miracle. Mom and I believe that we truly were given a gift, a miracle. God wants you to be happy, and He made our miracle possible.

We are so thankful God has shown us His power and His love. We are grateful every day that God gave Fluffy back to Mom. Maybe the antibiotics helped; maybe God put

Continued Miracles: Inspiring Testimonials

that other vet into our lives. We choose to believe our prayers were answered, and we were witnesses to an Easter miracle. Fluffy is happily playing at our house, and Mom loves her more than ever.

Your Response
What would you do if this were you?

Continued Miracles: Inspiring Testimonials

9

The Miracle of Salvation

It's not miracles that generate faith, but faith that generates miracles.
— Fyodor Dostoyevsky

Detoured (Debbie)

The Lord was on a mission today for souls, and I was scheduled for an appointment. He rearranged my schedule to fit His mission.

I quickly got dressed and put on my watch. I walked my dog, Juno—he wasn't happy that it was such a short walk, but I had to hurry. By the time I realized that my watch had broken, I was an hour late leaving for my appointment. I'd had no chance to read my Bible, other than my daily passage from Proverbs.

The bus was coming soon, so I kicked it into high gear. I grabbed my Bible tracts, locked the door, and ran down the tree-lined street to the bus stop. I stood on the curb, out of breath, as the bus approached on this noisy highway, and I waved my ball cap to signal the driver to stop.

I threw my blue book bag on the window seat next to me. The bus travelled to a major hub in the city, a fertile ground for those who didn't believe in the Lord, so I got out my tracts and put them on the seat. When I got off at my stop, I noticed two men giving out tracts on the street, and I nodded to them. Then I crossed at the traffic light and gave out my tracts on the other side.

When this God-appointment ended, I walked to the bus stop and placed my bag on the bench next to me. It's amazing who the Lord will bring to me, and it was about to happen again. I handed a tract to a young guy wearing shorts and a loose-fitting jersey with a college logo. On an impulse, I asked if he had stepped away from the Lord, and he replied, "Yes."

After we had talked for a few minutes, he leaned over the bench, grabbed my hand, closed his eyes, lowered his head and asked, "What do I need to do to be saved?" We prayed the prayer of salvation, and he gave his life to Christ. I gave him Scriptures, invited him to church, and told him God wanted him to turn his life around.

He jumped on his bus shortly afterward, and a clean looking young woman sat next to me in his spot. I gave her a tract, and she exclaimed, "I got this same tract on June 25, 2012." She said she had read the tract and signed the commitment for salvation at the end. She was thankful to receive a new copy of that tract because she had lost her wallet that contained the original one she signed. She shared her testimony with everyone nearby and asked for more tracts.

Reflecting on This Miracle

> For God so loved the world that he gave His only begotten Son, that whoever believes in Him should not perish but have everlasting life.
>
> —John 3:16

Your Response

Have you ever been given a gospel tract? Was it influential in your coming to faith in Christ?

Have you ever handed out tracts yourself? What were the results?

Breakthrough on Broad Street (Debbie)

Broad Street in Philadelphia booms with buses, cars, and foot traffic in the late afternoon. Over one and a half million people live in or travel to this historic city each day. People and buses are everywhere. When I stepped off the Philly bus after visiting the dentist, I trotted through the green light at Broad and Vine, jaunted across bustling Broad

Continued Miracles: Inspiring Testimonials

Street, and didn't waste time giving out tracts to passers-by and folks who were waiting for buses. The bus stop where I chose to wait has a pharmacy on the corner and is across from world renowned Hahnemann Hospital, a landmark in the Old City neighborhood of Philadelphia. The Lord had arranged an unexpected meeting for me on this corner.

I would become acquainted with Brandon, a young father who had just left work and crossed the street this sunny afternoon to wait for the bus on the same busy Philly corner as me. Smiling, I handed him my favorite tract entitled, "Let Not Your Heart Be Troubled," with its bright red heart on the cover. We chatted briefly, and I kept walking.

Later, I glanced around to see who read the tracts I had handed out. I was pleased that no one had thrown them on the ground. All of them had apparently been filed away in a pocket or purse—all but one. Brandon had his head down, reading his tract. The Lord chose to bless Brandon, and a seed was planted. I decided to make it a point to talk further with this young man.

What I didn't know was that, after I handed Brandon the tract, he thought, "This lady might help me change my life. God has sent me somebody to help me go forward." The Lord arranged for us to get on the same bus, and I asked to sit next to him. "I noticed you were reading the booklet I gave you," I said, hoping to begin a conversation. Brandon responded by telling me a bit about himself.

Reaching into my tote bag, I pulled out my old, marked-up, over-sized, well-worn King James Bible. It was falling apart, which is why it usually never left my house. I didn't know why I brought it with me that day. I showed him a few specific passages he could relate to and read every day.

Then I asked Brandon, "Are you ready to turn your life around? Would you like to give your life to the Lord?" He put his head down and replied, "Yes." He repeated the sinner's prayer slowly and pensively, and the Holy Spirit saved his soul while going over the Benjamin Franklin Bridge between Philadelphia and New Jersey.

Although Brandon had some issues, worries, and sadness in his life, I was encouraged as I spoke to him that his commitment was going to be a lasting one. We discussed what his next steps would be: attending a church, getting baptized, and studying the Word of God.

I gave Brandon my information before he left the bus, and I silently asked the Lord to send someone into his path to help him. I didn't know if I would see him again, so I gave him a hug. Coming from a woman twice his age that hug may have seemed a little awkward, but it was an important connection for Brandon. He had a lot going on in his life, and he needed the love and support. He looked a bit stunned as he left the bus, but then I had given him a lot to think about. He told me that his next goal was to be baptized.

The following Wednesday morning I travelled to Broad Street to go back to the dentist for another appointment. Guess who rode the early morning bus with me a second time? Brandon saw me speaking with the bus driver and recognized my signature hot-pink baseball cap. He came forward from the back of the bus, smiled, and spoke to me briefly. He made it a point to give me a hug after we both exited the bus at Broad Street.

When I asked Brandon if he would like a Bible and if he would read it, he said yes. I asked him where he worked in case he wasn't at the bus stop when I returned. I said I would bring him a Bible, but I didn't know when. (I wasn't scheduled to go to the dentist for two more weeks.) He came forward for another hug.

Who would believe the Lord would decide I would be the one to help Brandon? How wonderful—and yet, where and when would I see Brandon to give him a Bible?

The next Thursday afternoon was sunny. I walked to the bus stop about a mile from the house and made a special

Continued Miracles: Inspiring Testimonials

trip into the city to give Brandon his Bible. Would I have trouble finding him? When the bus arrived at the stop where we first met, I looked for him, but didn't see him. I didn't give up and decided to seek Brandon at work. When the bus doors opened at the stop near Brandon's workplace, my eyes grew wide and my mouth dropped open. Brandon stood on the curb with a bag of new toys. We were both amazed—Praise God! I never got off the bus; Brandon got on, and I paid the same driver for a return trip. The Lord reserved the two front seats for us.

I handed Brandon his new NIV Bible, and we sat for a Bible lesson together. He smiled, expressing gratitude that a stranger would take the time to mentor him. He told me his sister was a believer and attended church in another area in New Jersey. When we got near Brandon's destination, I suggested he try a small church on the corner, two blocks from his house. I knew the pastors personally, so I later contacted them and asked them to look for him.
Thank you, Holy Spirit!

Since then I've seen Brandon a few more times, and we have become friends. The last time I checked with him, he was still reading the Bible on his own, but due to his work schedule he wasn't attending church. Brandon was touched when one of the families from our church treated him and his son to a big bag of wrapped Christmas presents, which I delivered to him on the bus. He gave me a big smile and a hug.

Reflecting on This Miracle

> For the Son of man has come to seek and save that which was lost.
>
> —Luke 19:10

Brandon's Reflections

There's always going to be somebody to help you if you're willing to accept help. It's been almost three years since I first met Debbie. After that first meeting, I had a dream that I would see her again, but I wasn't sure it would really happen since she didn't live or work near me. God put her in my path again on the same street corner, at the same time, and on the same bus.

My faith is growing stronger all the time. We just had a Bible study at work during break time. I like the Christian books I've been given. I read one story about worrying, and I applied it right away to my work situation.

Continued Miracles: Inspiring Testimonials

Your Response

Would you step out of your comfort zone to ask a stranger to sit with you on the bus? Would you be willing to ask someone if they needed a Bible?

God Behind the Scenes (Debbie)

On a hot Saturday in July, I volunteered to help at a ministry outreach in Philadelphia, serving food and handing out clothing to the disadvantaged. My attention focused on serving the people in line, but God directed my attention to a woman and her young son, sitting behind me on a bench and exhausted from the heat.

I felt led by God to ask the woman why they were sitting on the bench. She replied that she only came to get a Bible. She began to share some of her challenges, as well as some of the hardships she faced. As I listened, God gave me the words to say to her, and she received Christ. It was a miracle. She and her son "not" only received a Bible and food, but a spiritual transformation that spoke life into her dead situation.

Reflecting on This Miracle

> Beloved, let us love one another; for love is of God; and everyone who loves is born of God and knows God.

Continued Miracles: Inspiring Testimonials

—1 John 4:7

Your Response

Have you ever been impressed to talk about Christ to a stranger? How would you begin such a conversation?

From Prison to Praise (José)

I really did it this time, I said to myself disgustedly. It was 2:30 a.m., and police vehicles surrounded my car with bright lights flashing as I clenched the wheel. The officer standing at my window yelled, "Get out of the car with your hands up." When I stepped out, he threw me against the hood and demanded, "Where is the gun?"

I replied, "I don't know," even though I knew it was under the driver's seat. The officer found it quickly and slammed the door shut. Then they beat me, handcuffed me, and threw me in the back of the squad car.

I heard the gavel bang on the judge's desk as she issued a sentence of two-and-a-half to ten years for armed robbery. I was just twenty-one years old at the time. I raised my hand and asked her if she would be so kind as to reconsider to which she replied, "No."

For the first time in my life, I accepted the punishment and didn't throw a fit. I heard my mother and my family crying, and I was sad because I hurt them. As I was taken in cuffs to a holding cell in the basement of the court house, I heard two police officers comment that I shouldn't have been sentenced so harshly.

I was escorted downstairs in an elevator to get processed when another prisoner entered, accompanied by a guard. The prisoner asked me how long of a sentence I received. When I told him, he said, "I got fifteen to thirty, but God is good."

I just looked at him and said, "You're crazy. You're out of your mind." This was the first time God made His presence known to me.

I was taken to a correctional facility where I was put in a quarantine area. In the holding cell I slept on the floor next to the toilet because of overcrowding. God allowed me to be broken; He was pruning me. A female guard opened the slatted door and said, "I can only take two of you." My name was the second to be called.

I was taken to my cell where I met Enoch, one of the prisoners I had seen in the courthouse. I saw him with a book and asked, "What are you reading?"

"The Bible," he replied, "and I'm surprised they let me in with it." I asked him if I could read from his Bible, and

Continued Miracles: Inspiring Testimonials

I read the Gospel of Matthew out loud for everyone my first night. My two cellmates that night were Enoch and a younger man, Jason.

Later, I was assigned and driven to another county jail in Philadelphia where I also had two cellmates, one a man of another faith and one a young kid. I threw my stuff on the bed the first day and over the public address system I heard, "Church line." I hopped in the line. I kept asking for a Bible with the excuse that I wanted something to read.

One guy in line said, "Here, take this Bible. I've got another in the cell." When I glanced around, no one else had one. After I got back to my cell, I didn't read it right away. My cellmate, who was of a different faith, opened my Bible and began interpreting the first chapter of Genesis according to his beliefs. I just ignored him.

I moved to another cell and was given the job of cooking meals for the men. I was happy to don a chef's uniform and have a taste of freedom in the kitchen. I loved the aroma of the chicken cooking, and I learned how to cook large-volume meals. My new cellmate was very religious and of a different faith, and for various reasons we didn't always get along.

Continued Miracles: Inspiring Testimonials

One day at 4 a.m. a guard knocked at my metal cell door and said, "Figueroa, pack up your stuff." The box he handed me was labeled SCI-G (State Correctional Institution Graterford, Pennsylvania's largest maximum security prison, about thirty miles outside of Philadelphia). I stood in line chained to at least fifty men around the waist, legs, and arms, waiting to go on the transport bus. As we approached the facility, the first thing in view when the sun came up was a thirty-foot concrete wall surrounding the prison and two strong guards carrying a body bag out the front door. This left a first and lasting impression.

All my belongings had been thrown away except my Bible, toothbrush, and a few necessary things. I was scared, curious, and missing my family. After I got to my cell and the door clanged closed, I met my cellmate, threw my stuff on the bunk, and wept rivers.

Then I heard someone say, "Trust me. Trust me." I grabbed my Bible and knew the Lord spoke to me. I read the whole Bible in nine days in between fasting off and on and going out in the yard for fresh air and sunshine.

The second morning at Graterford, I got on my knees and declared, "God, if You're real, show me. I don't want to learn from someone else. I want You to reveal Yourself to me." And that day He did reveal Himself to me. I received

Continued Miracles: Inspiring Testimonials

His comfort and started a relationship with Him. I was surprised to find that so many men at Graterford had very long sentences. Out in the yard I met a couple of other believers— William, who used to be a pastor, and Joe, who just received a life sentence. William and Joe would preach to us, and I admired the way they spoke. They used to tell me, "You think we're a blessing? You're a blessing to us since you bring us fresh revelation from the Lord."

Eventually, I was moved to State Correctional Institution Camp Hill near Harrisburg. There were seventy five of us who were in line for another quarantine. Because of the odd number of men, my name was the last one to be called to receive my cell. For the first time since my incarceration, I was alone in my cell for twenty-three hours a day for three days straight. I told God, "I can't do this." I spent hours reading my Bible, falling asleep, or looking out the window.

Then, the small speaker by the door sounded my name and offered me the job of Tier Worker. I accepted the position and was moved to another cell. Joy overtook me because this job meant I could take a real shower more than a minute long. My duties included cleaning and handing out meals and blankets to new men. I was assigned to a new cell block where I remained for the rest of my stay.

Continued Miracles: Inspiring Testimonials

I was glad to get more privileges. I bought a television and food from the commissary. I was allowed four-hour visits with my family, and I shared the gospel. The sheet of activities I was given included a Bible study, and I decided to go.

When I arrived at the chapel for the Bible study, it was already in progress. Forty men attended. We were asked if anyone wanted to share a testimony. I agreed. As I was telling my testimony, I shared about the Christian brothers I had met along the way. As I glanced at the men in the front row, I was speechless.

Pedro (the first Christian I met in the courthouse elevator) sat there as well as Enoch (the cellmate who let me read his Bible), Jonah (the man in line who gave me his Bible), and William and Joe (the two preachers). My face lit up with the biggest smile since I entered the prison system. I hugged each one. The Lord was showing me His presence, and I smiled overjoyed.

I also met Ramon, another believer on my block. He was a powerful prophet of God whom I spent time with after the brothers transferred to other prisons. We got close to the chaplain and were allowed to go down to see him. I was also blessed to be given a "visiting" job which allowed me to interact with people who came to the facility.

One day I spoke with the chaplain when I noticed another prisoner walking with a cane. I heard, "Healing." I looked at the man with the cane and said sarcastically, "Lord, I know you're not asking me to heal him." I left the office and walked into the main corridor, pulled the guy with the cane aside, and told him, "You can't receive healing from someone you don't believe in." Then I led him in the prayer of salvation.

Afterward, I asked him to follow me back to the chaplain's office, we placed our hands on his shoulder, and I asked the chaplain to lead us in prayer. I allowed the Spirit to take over, and I started speaking in tongues. I felt intense heat as I held the man's back and knee. Once the prayer ended, his pain disappeared.

This was the first miracle I ever witnessed. The man got excited and shocked because he didn't have to use his cane. He accepted a Bible from the chaplain and promised to continue searching for the Lord. I didn't know what to think. I just kept thanking the Lord for sticking to his Word. A year and a half later, I was released from Camp Hill. I found that readjusting to life outside prison was a challenge because of the many temptations. But I kept reading my Bible and calling on the Lord. Now I know the Lord used the prison experience to mold me.

Reflecting on This Miracle

> I beseech you therefore, brethren, by the mercies of God, that you present your bodies a living sacrifice, holy, acceptable to God, which is your reasonable service. And do not be conformed to this world, but be transformed by the renewing of your mind, that you may prove what is that good and acceptable and perfect will of God.
>
> —Romans 12:1-2

Jose's Reflections

You never know who the Lord will put in your path to help you. I take the Word of God literally and seriously. Even though it may be hard when you go through obstacles, God will always continue to move on your behalf if you stay in the right position. Continue to seek Him on a regular basis even on good days.

Today I am a productive member of society. I share the Word of God from the Bible and lead people to Christ.

Continued Miracles: Inspiring Testimonials

Your Response

You may not be able to read the Bible in nine days like Jose, but are you consistent in reading the Bible? Do you have a friend who can help keep you on track?

Weigh No More (Rosemary)

Though I was pretty as a child with big green eyes, a cute smile, and long, brown, curly hair, students often ridiculed me at school. When I had to wear a patch over my left eye for a period of time, the kids made fun of me. When I developed a stutter in the seventh grade, they teased me unmercifully. But while those were only temporary embarrassments, most of the time they singled me out for jokes and mean comments about being overweight.

My insecurities stopped me from pursuing the dreams I had of a glamorous career as a model, a flight attendant, or an actress. I often stifled my ambitions, my opinions, and my interest in other people because of these early experiences.

As I grew older, however, I became stronger and more outgoing. I stood to people and—diplomatically—expressing how I felt about circumstances. My life became relatively normal. Though I became somewhat obsessed with dieting and exercise, I had a great husband, a good job, and a nice home, but something was missing. I just didn't know What.

One fall day I wanted to bask in the beauty of the trees and quiet of the land, so I drove down to the old Delaware Canal outside Yardley, Pennsylvania. As I trotted next to the gleaming water, I heard a still small voice say, "You are going to find something dead and moving."

Immediately, I looked to the right; there in the water lay a groundhog. It was dead, but it was moving, carried along by the meandering current. *Why would I say that to myself?* I thought. *What does it mean?*

Five months later I was working out at the gym. While lying on my stomach doing leg lifts, I heard *that* voice again: "You have to lose weight and learn the Bible." *I know I should lose weight,* I thought, *but what is this about learning the Bible? Where is this voice coming from? What is going on?*

About five minutes later, I heard the voice yet again: "You must touch that man." I looked around the gym and saw only one man there on a treadmill with oxygen hooked up to his nose. I said to myself, "I will *not* touch that man." About ten minutes after I heard that strange command, the man left. I finished and left the gym about twenty minutes later.

My next errand took me to the grocery store, but before backing my car out of the parking spot at the gym, I tuned my radio to a Christian station, instead of my usual country music.

I listened to a testimony by Bob, a railroad worker who had been crushed between two trains that had rolled together. Bob went through two unsuccessful cervical fusions of the spinal cord, and then he was diagnosed with cancer. This man almost gave up after six years of pain and suffering. He wanted to die, but he was led into a Christian counseling ministry where he found a purpose for living. He quoted Romans 8:18: "I consider that our present sufferings are not worth comparing with the glory that will be revealed in us."

As I pulled my car into the grocery store parking lot, I turned off the engine but kept the radio on. I began to relate immediately to Bob—though I had not experienced his physical pain, I had put myself through tremendous mental anguish. I made many wrong choices in my life that led me down one-way roads where I could not turn around. My hopelessness became so heavy I felt my whole world would collapse under me.

But listening to Bob's testimony, I began to feel my spirit changing. Though I was alone in the car, I felt a presence. I felt peace instead of insecurity and worthlessness. The pressures in my life lifted off my shoulders. Tears flowed uncontrollably down my cheeks. God transformed me into a child of God who would follow Him forever. Through foggy windows I listened and comprehended words from the Bible I heard before such as, "His divine power has given us everything we need for life and godliness through him who called us by his own glory and goodness" (2 Peter 1:3).

But why me? Why was I given the keys to eternal life? I had so many sins on my list God was probably tired of turning the pages. I began to pray and thank God for His overflowing love. Was this what I had been looking for? I always thought I had to earn His approval by what I achieved in life.

I began to wonder what would happen once I opened the car door. Would this feeling go away when I left the inner sanctuary of my car? Would I still feel the same? I finally stepped out of my car, stood up, and raised my hands to the sky. I exclaimed, "This is truly the first day of the rest of my life."

Continued Miracles: Inspiring Testimonials

As I walked toward the store in the presence of my Father, I said inwardly, "Lord, please let me live at least another forty-three years so I can have another lifetime with You." When I sauntered into the store, everyone seemed to turn and smile at me. I saw everything with clean, fresh eyes. The colors in the store were amazingly bright, and the fruits and vegetables were glistening. I felt as though I had just come from a third-world country and was being introduced to a grocery store for the first time.

What bounty we have, I thought.

While looking over the mushrooms, I heard another voice come from the silence: "Did you have a good workout?"

I turned around to see the man from the gym. Gently, I put my hand on his arm and replied, "You have no idea what kind of a workout I just had."

"I'm glad you had a good one. See you around," he said and walked on.

"Have a good evening," I said with a smile. God had confirmed that He was speaking to me earlier at the gym. I couldn't have been more blessed and thrilled.

Later that day, I began humming to myself, experiencing the birthday feeling I used to get when I was a kid. Actually, this was my birthday—my born-again birthday! I had an angelic honeymoon with the Lord for many days. I found a Christian bookstore and bought my first Bible and devotional. I began to immerse myself in reading the Bible more each day.

I also realized why God told me I was going to find "something dead and moving." God was showing me a picture of myself—dead in my spirit but moving through life. Not anymore.

Let Him give you light so you can see His glory.

Reflecting on This Miracle

> I have taught you in the way of wisdom; I have led you in right paths. When you walk, your steps will not be hindered, and when you run, you will not stumble.
>
> —Proverbs 4:11-12

Rosemary's Reflections

I speak to the Lord daily in my own words since I know He is with me constantly. Also, reading the Bible is extremely important to me. I watch Christian television and listen to Christian radio stations. I receive so much hope through these venues. If you receive Jesus in your heart, He will guide and direct you if you let Him.

Rosemary's full story can be read in her book, *Dead and Moving*.

Your Response

Have you found the joy of a relationship with God as Rosemary did? Are you willing to share your testimony?

10
Miscellaneous

When others doubt the power of Jesus, be the one who asks Him to perform the impossible. He often will.
— Dillon Burroughs

Holy Trinity House of Prayer (Pastor Curtis Williams)

God gave me a vision to start a church. He also gave me the name of the church, one-and-a-half years before it opened. The church started out in my home and grew until God showed me a building in Browns Mill, New Jersey.

We didn't experience any issues in acquiring the building. God blessed Holy Trinity House of Prayer with financial and staff support. My staff and I had to approach the township zoning board before the doors could open. We went to the township three or four times to get a hearing, but the meeting was postponed or canceled each time.

When launching a church, spiritual warfare is a factor. The last night the hearing was scheduled, only five of the eight members were in attendance. Township policy stated that if one of the five members present voted against the church, the request would be denied.

God touched the heart of each board member. The township granted unanimous approval, and the building met specified zoning qualifications. God was faithful, and He opened the doors of the church. Holy Trinity House of Prayer has been in its own building for several years now. All visitors receive a warm welcome.

Reflecting on This Miracle

> Even them I will bring to My holy mountain and make them joyful in My house of prayer. Their burnt offerings and their sacrifices will be accepted on my altar; for my house shall be called a house of prayer for all nations.
>
> —Isaiah 56:7

Pastor William's Reflections

Nothing is too hard for the Lord.

Your Response

Have you ever experienced spiritual warfare? How did you respond?

Seeing is Believing (Ray)

College life can be both fun and stressful. It certainly was for me. I felt overwhelmed with courses, tests, and a

Continued Miracles: Inspiring Testimonials

hectic routine. I had a full agenda, and like many other college students, I didn't go to church, and I didn't own a Bible.

So what happened to me next was a real eye opener!

One night, under immense stress, I called out to God. "God, show me a sign that You are real." I'm not sure what I was expecting, but I didn't see or hear anything different, and I went to bed, still stressed. The next morning, I woke up and went about my routine. But when I opened the front door, I was stunned.

I looked down at the doorstep and saw a new Bible. Was this a dream? I had struggled with reaching out to God because He wasn't tangible. Now I had the tangible proof that an unbeliever needed. I didn't know who had brought this new Bible. All I knew was that God didn't bring me a big screen TV or an iPad—He brought me His Word.

I shared this miracle with just a few other people because I figured most of my college friends probably weren't interested in my story. They just wouldn't relate.

Owning a Bible wasn't the "in" thing. But I kept that Bible for years and read it.

Today I am more fluent in God's Word, and I have begun attending church. My experience has positively influenced me. Now I am able to discuss the Bible with others. My favorite selections in the Bible are from the book of Proverbs.

Reflecting on This Miracle

> Jesus said to Him, "If you can believe, all things are possible to him who believes." Immediately, the father of the child cried out and said with tears,
>
> "Lord, I believe; help my unbelief."
>
> —Mark 9:23-24

Ray's Reflections

God wants you to believe in Him even if you can't see Him.

Your Response

If you were a college student like Ray, do you think a Bible appearing at your door would have led you to faith?

11

Write Your Own Miracle Story

Miracles are delivered but are not always welcome.
—Debra L. Stout

Why should I write my own miracle story?

Your miracle was never created just for you. God meant it as a testimony to share with others, to give them a ray of hope, and to give Him the glory. You've probably had many miracles over the years. You've heard, read, and been encouraged by others' miracles. Now it's your turn, if you so choose, to detail your miracle as a keepsake. Many details are lost over time if a story isn't kept fresh and told repeatedly. Use this template to get started.

My Own Miracle Story

Title of my miracle:

Issue and details:

How was I feeling before my miracle?

When did my issue start and end?

Did I thank God for my miracle, or did I think my issue was just resolved by natural means?

Continued Miracles: Inspiring Testimonials

How did my miracle affect my belief, faith, and trust in God?
Scripture that applies to my miracle:
What would I like someone else to learn from my miracle?
With whom have you shared your miracle story so far?
What was the outcome?

Did I miss my miracle? Think. A coincidence is not a miracle and a miracle is not a coincidence. Be on the lookout for your miracle. God isn't going to text you.

You may have experienced a miracle, your aha moment, and didn't know it. Have you ever had a positive situation where something happened to you or for you that you didn't have a reasonable explanation for, you didn't expect, and wasn't within your control to produce the result? This could be your miracle. It doesn't have to be as sensational as discovering a baby alive under rubble after an earthquake.

12
Seven Catalysts to Your Miracle

I thought it good to declare the signs and wonders that the Most High God has worked for me. How great are his signs, And how mighty are his wonders! His kingdom is an everlasting kingdom, and His dominion is from generation to generation.

—Daniel 4:2-3

Seven Catalysts to Your Miracle

Why do you want a miracle? To experience God? Then pray to God for your miracle and be specific. If He detects you are not sincere in believing for your miracle, guess what? God determines who gets miracles.

1. Believe the Lord for your miracle. Read Acts 15:12, John 2:23, 20:29.

2. Receive your miracle gratefully, and receive your miracle right now.

3. Give the Lord thanks sooner rather than later. Thank Him every day before receiving your miracle, when it happens, and long after. Give Him the glory.

4. Get yourself out of the way. Don't let your issues dominate you. Keep your focus on the Lord instead

5. Read miracles in the Bible. Find the miracles in the Bible, and then read and re-read them. They were written for our benefit and are still relevant today.
6. Share your testimony. Your miracle was not meant only for you. When you share your testimony, you never know who may say, "I needed that."
7. Pray. Pray. Pray.

Conclusion: Seeking God

Everybody wants a miracle; we just don't want to be in a situation where we need one. You can't have one without the other. Sometimes what we perceive as our problem is really God setting us up to do something miraculous in our lives. It's about training ourselves to see those problems as opportunities so God can intervene.
— Mark Batterson

Paul, a friend of mine who is an evangelist, has an important message for us about the purpose of miracles in our lives, and I cannot think of a better way to conclude this book. May the Lord richly bless you with a miracle.
— **Debra L. Stout**

The purpose of these testimonies is to reveal that God does do miracles and He is real. But how can you get God to do miracles in your life? What if I told you there is a certain way to open yourself up to the supernatural and a way to have an actual relationship with the Creator of Life? Your prayers can get answered. He guides you in life, and you have real faith you can touch and feel supernaturally. What if I told you this is the way God designed it and wanted it all along? How do we do this?

God wants us to seek Him. The world looks at God through human eyes. If God were this ... If God were that

… He would do… The reality is God doesn't change for us. We have to change for Him. "But from there you will seek the Lord your God, and you will find Him if you seek Him with all your heart and soul." (Dueteronomy 4:29). God is right here with us, always waiting for us to reach out to Him. This is why a lot of people find God when they are broken. Most people truly call out to God and say, "If You're real, show me." If you really have a desire to know God, tell Him. He is all around you and knows your thoughts. Ask Him to reveal Himself to you. Call out to Him until he starts answering you. It doesn't always happen immediately. Talk to Him. Pray to Him day after day even if it's a few minutes here and there but be sincere in your heart about finding Him. Everyone who is sincere in their heart will find God when they seek Him. "And ye shall seek me and find me, when ye see me with all your heart. (Jeremiah 29:13)

Prayer is your communication with God. But how do you hear back from God? God can speak to you through circumstances in your life, through other people, through dreams and visions, but mainly, through His Word. If you're truly seeking God, pick up a Bible, and ask Him to reveal Himself to you. Flip the Bible open and start reading. The Bible is the Word of God, written by man but inspired by the

Holy Spirit. "For the Word of God is living and powerful, and sharper than any two edged sword, piercing even to the division of soul and spirit, and of joint and marrow, and is a discerner of heart" (Hebrews 4:12). A true Christian with real faith will tell you that the Bible can speak to your thoughts. This is the living Word of God! It is God speaking back to you, and that is miraculous! That is the start of your-faith to be able to receive miracles from God.

You can have a relationship with God, the Creator of life through Christ. You talk; He listens; He answers you. You learn how to listen to Him and how to talk to Him through the Bible. This is the Bible's purpose. The Bible teaches us how to have a relationship with God, which is the reason we were created. We lost that relationship because of some sin. Some people try to fill the void or loss of relationship with money, drugs, alcohol, and human relationships.

God came in the flesh to be the perfect sacrifice for our sins and to get our relationship with God back to the way He originally intended it to be. (See 2 Timothy 3:16) The purpose was so that we could receive forgiveness from God. "Then Peter said unto them. Repent and be baptized every one of you in the name of Jesus Christ for the remission of sins and ye shall receive the Gift of the Holy Ghost" (Acts 2:38). "Blessed are they which do hunger and thirst after righteousness for they shall be filled" (Matthew 5:6).

When you truly become indwelled by the Spirit of God, you will feel it. This is the biggest miracle of all-the ability to have eternal life and to receive God's Spirit inside you, touching you, and changing you. But to get there we need faith.

Hearing God's Word is how our faith starts. "So then faith cometh by hearing and hearing by the word of God." (Romans 10:17)

Listening to God says to us in our daily life is how miracles start. When He talks, He tells us what to do in our present situation with our job, health, or relationships. Our part is to obey. He comes into our lives with His power to change our situation. Everything starts with us hearing from our God.

Ask God to come into your life. Seek Him. Then look for His answers and follow His directives. God will start doing miracles in your life.

May God bless you with the miracle of salvation.

Endnotes

1. "Miracle," Definition 1, *Harper's Bible Dictionary*. Paul L. Achtemeir, ed. San Francisco: Harper & Row, Publishers,1985.
2. "Roosevelt Boulevard (Philadelphia)." *Wikipedia*. Wikimedia Foundation, Inc. Online at http;//en.wikipedia.org/wiki/Roosevelt_Boulevard_%28Phi ladelphia%29.
Date accessed: 15 February 2014.

Continued Miracle: Inspiring Testimonials

ABOUT THE AUTHOR

Debra Stout (Debbie) Entrepreneur, Educator, and Author of the book entitled, *"Continued Miracles— Inspiring Testimonies of God at Work in the Lives of Everyday People"* and the children's book series *"Juno Stories."* She is a strong believer in God's supernatural realm of miracles, a speaker for the Lord, and leads weekly Bible Study.

Debra's international outreach includes cross-cultural ministry on the top of the mountains in Tijuana, Mexico. She has a sincere passion for those who are homeless and in need of food and shelter.

Debra's unique perspective is a combination of leadership, compassion, and academia creating a message for all to enjoy.

Visit us at continuedmiracles.com

Continued Miracle: Inspiring Testimonials

www.ingramcontent.com/pod-product-compliance
Lightning Source LLC
LaVergne TN
LVHW051116080426
835510LV00018B/2067